MADAME TUSSAUD IN ENGLAND

Career Woman Extraordinary

MADAME TUSSAUD
IN ENGLAND

Career Woman Extraordinary

Pauline Chapman

QUILLER PRESS
London

First published 1992
by Quiller Press Ltd
46 Lillie Road
London SW6 1TN

Copyright © 1992 Pauline Chapman

ISBN 870948-79-3

Produced by Hugh Tempest-Radford *Book Producers*

Typesetting by Galleon Photosetting, Ipswich
Printed and bound in Great Britain

Contents

List of Illustrations

In the text

Between pages 86 and 87

1 Portrait of Dr Philippe Curtius in his National Guard uniform by Gilles Louis Chrétien, circa 1790.

2 Portrait of Madame Tussaud in middle-age. Artist unknown.

3 Portrait bust of Francis Tussaud, Madame Tussaud's second son, born 1800.

4 Portrait of Joseph Tussaud, Madame Tussaud's elder son, born 1798.

5 Family group of silhouettes by Joseph Tussaud.

6 View of Edinburgh in 1803 when Madame Tussaud's exhibition paid its first visit.

7 The Grand Assembly Room, York. A typical venue for the showing of Madame Tussaud's exhibition.

8 The Bristol Riots 1831 showing Madame Tussaud's figures being carried out of the Assembly Rooms to save them from fire. Watercolour by William Muller.

9 Engraving of 'The Green Man', Blackheath, where Madame Tussaud set up her exhibition in 1835.

10 Engraving of the Market Place, Hull, where Madame Tussaud's exhibition was shown in 1826.

11 Tableau of George IV and his Coronation robes in Madame Tussaud's exhibition at Bazaar, Baker Street. Engraving from Mead's 'London Interiors', 1840.

12 Sketch showing seating for visitors in the Great Room of Madame Tussaud's exhibition at Bazaar, Baker Street, 1842.

13 Engraving showing the vista and elaborate decoration of the Great Room, Bazaar, Baker Street, in 1840.

14 Cartoon of the Chamber of Horrors in Madame Tussaud's exhibition with article from *Punch*, 1849.

15 John Theodore Tussaud, great-grandson of Madame Tussaud, in his studio.

16 The Napoleon Group added to Madame Tussaud's exhibition, Marylebone Road in 1888.

Acknowledgements

The author's thanks and gratitude go to Madame Tussaud's Ltd for allowing use of their archive material, and also to the many local history librarians who have helped to trace material relating to Madame Tussaud's years of travel and her London exhibition.

INTRODUCTION

The Background

———◆———

MADAME Tussaud (1761–1850) was nearly forty-two years old when she brought her exhibition of wax figures to England. No contemporary description of her indicates the inflexible will and determination that lay beneath her 'amiable' appearance and manner, nor that she would found here, single-handed, a source of entertainment and knowledge that, 190 years after its first presentation in London, would still attract vast numbers of visitors from all over the world.

As a girl Marie Grosholtz, as she then was, had been called pretty by Maximilien Robespierre, instigator of the French Revolutionary Terror. To the English public she appeared, in her middle years, typically French, vivacious and voluble, always ready with an anecdote. Very small in stature, with dark hair and eyes and a prominent nose – her 'Bourbon nose' as her descendants called it, though there is no evidence of Bourbon blood – she aged into 'dear old Madame Tussaud'. She showed no scars from the terrible experiences during the French Revolution that had steeled her character, yet never attempted to conceal or minimise them. They became, in fact, a vital part of her stock-in-trade.

Marie Grosholtz had grown up in Paris under the roof and tutelage of the man she called 'uncle' for whom her mother worked as housekeeper. Her remarkable talent for wax modelling was evident from the age of six, when Dr Philippe Curtius, founder and proprietor of the famous *Salon de Cire* began to train her in his own expertise and skill as a sculptor of wax.

It was a show business world in which she lived till the age of eighteen, exciting and interesting amid the splendours and squalors of pre-Revolutionary Paris. Visitors of all nationalities came to Curtius's wax exhibition which was always updated to reflect contemporary events and personalities, political and otherwise. Royal visitors included Madame Elizabeth, sister of King Louis XVI, who took a

1

fancy to this talented young artist and invited her to join her household at Versailles as art tutor. Madame Elizabeth, who had artistic abilities – her embroidery was of almost professional standard – wished to learn something of modelling in the fashionable medium of wax.

Such an offer could not possibly be refused and Marie was not daunted by it. She was already accustomed to meeting members of Royal families and persons of high rank. From quite an early age she had stood at Curtius's side and assisted when he ceremoniously welcomed and showed round important visitors. She had learned from him to be discreet in her remarks, and easy and pleasant as well as respectful when in exalted company.

As a member of Madame Elizabeth's household Marie often had access to Court functions. She learned Court manners while her sharp intelligence observed the intrigues, the rivalries, and the relentless quest for pleasure and profit which characterized Court life at Versailles. She had ample opportunity to practise her art, which brought her into contact with Ministers, officials, and courtiers who were eager to sit for the Princess's art tutor for their portraits in wax.

In Madame Elizabeth's private apartments Marie even had personal contact with members of the Royal Family of France, including King Louis XVI and Queen Marie Antoinette who paid frequent informal visits. They were always courteous and friendly in manner when they noticed the little figure of the art tutor in the room. To Madame Elizabeth herself, three years younger than Marie, she became gradually a friend as far as the difference in their status would permit. Marie, already experienced in the running and accounting of the *Salon de Cire*, was competent to advise on and help organize the many charitable donations that flowed from Madame Elizabeth's limited purse. At the same time Marie was given enough liberty to pay frequent visits to her 'uncle' Curtius and mother in the Boulevard du Temple and even to do some modelling for the exhibition there.

So the years passed and Marie held her position at Versailles until early in 1789. She was now a capable young woman of twenty-eight, well experienced in her art. Then Curtius, who had cultivated a considerable number of political friends and contacts, many of whom he entertained at his excellent table, judged that revolution was inevitable and close at hand. He petitioned for Marie's release from Royal service. She returned to live under his roof and resumed her full activities in the exhibition. It was not too soon.

On 12 July the news got round that the King had dismissed Finance Minister Necker, and banished his relative the Duc d' Orléans, both of whom were urging reform. Riots broke out in Paris. Curtius's wax likenesses were celebrated and a crowd of angry men and women marched to the exhibition determined to seize those of Necker and the Duc d'Orléans to parade them round the streets in a protest march. Curtius, faced with their demands, handed them over without demur, though he did persuade the leaders of the mob to leave the full-length figures of the King and Queen which they also wished to seize. Revolution came two days later on 14 July 1789, with the storming of the Bastille, that formidable prison-fortress in the centre of Paris, by an infuriated mob.

When rumours of the attack reached Curtius, he left to collect and lead his squad of men in the newly formed National Guard of which he was an active member as Captain of the district battalion. Marie remained at the exhibition. She did not know what was happening at the Bastille but in a few hours she was to learn.

The mob had seized the Governor of the Bastille, de Launay, an old man, and dragged him to the Hôtel de Ville. They also seized Flesselles, the Provost of the Merchants, representative of the Paris Guilds. In the fury of the crowd both prisoners were decapitated. The heads were stuck on pikes. Someone in the crowd shouted, 'Take them to Curtius', and the mob set off for the Boulevard du Temple not far away. Marie saw them coming, carrying something aloft on pikes. She had no idea where Curtius was and came out to face the men as they jostled to the door.

The decision Marie faced was terrible. Should she run inside and lock the door? That could well mean the wrecking of the exhibition; probably they would burn it, and, seeing the temper of the mob, massacre her mother and the staff who were within. Or should she steel herself, take the bleeding heads on to her lap, and spread the plaster for the death masks, promising the wax portraits would be quickly finished? She steeled herself and fetched the materials. A passing eyewitness saw her sitting there, outside the door, performing the task she was faced with. She did not know that these two severed heads were only the first death heads she would have to create in wax. It was in September 1792 that enraged and bloodthirsty mobs broke into the prisons of Paris, massacring the inmates who they believed to be aristocrats and priests. Among these victims was the Princesse de Lamballe, one-time intimate friend of Queen Marie Antoinette. Marie had known her well at Versailles, but dared not show her horror when she had to work on those charming and gentle features before the severed head was again carried off on a pike to be displayed beneath the windows of the Queen, now a prisoner in the Temple.

The death heads Marie had modelled under threat from her fellow-citizens led to an official command from the Revolutionary authority. She was ordered in January 1793 to make a secret visit to the cemetery of the Madeleine Church and take a death mask from the head of King Louis XVI before it was thrown into a common grave after his execution. In July of the same year, again under command, she made her way to the house of Marat who lay assassinated in his bath, stabbed by a young woman from Normandy who believed that in killing this monster she was saving France from further horrors. In October Marie was again at the Madeleine cemetery, this time with the head of Marie Antoinette on her lap. By now she had ceased to feel fear. She did what she was compelled to do.

Revolutionary leaders rose and fell. By 1794 Robespierre had seized power and instigated the Terror. Curtius, who had known Robespierre for a long time, found himself involved in political matters and was despatched on several missions to the Rhineland where, as a fluent German speaker, he could carry out some useful inspection duties. It was while he was away, in the early summer of 1794, that Marie and her mother were suddenly arrested and taken to prison, denounced by some unknown local enemy. Such imprisonment was the first step to the guillotine. Marie and her mother were saved only by the overthrow of Robespierre and the end of the Terror, when prison gates were opened and most of those packed inside were set free. Scarcely was she back at the Boulevard du Temple when orders came again from those now holding power. Marie took the death mask of Robespierre's guillotined head, with a gunshot wound in the jaw, possibly self-inflicted. Even then Marie's gruesome labours were not finished. She had to deal, under the usual compulsion, with the death heads of Carrier, notorious for his mass drowning of suspects in the river at Nantes, and Fouquier-Tinville, former Public Prosecutor, who was said to have gained much personal pleasure by sending people to their death on the guillotine.

Curtius had returned from the Rhineland in ill-health, after the fall of Robespierre. He did not rally and a great personal loss struck Marie in the autumn of 1794 with the death of this man, who had been her teacher and mentor since she was a child. Marie always believed he had been poisoned. In treading his wary path through the Revolutionary years, and when on his missions he had made enemies. He left her the *Salon de Cire* and all his property in his will, calling her 'my pupil in my art'. She lost her teacher and mentor, but his influence remained the dominating factor in her life, and the preservation of the exhibition he had founded her unflinching determination.

In 1795 Marie became Madame Tussaud, marrying a civil engineer some eight years younger than herself. As the years passed, she realised that her marriage had not been a wise move. Her husband proved irresponsible. While Marie earned the money in the *Salon de Cire* he liked to speculate unsuccessfully in theatrical property. Tastes were changing too and the exhibition waned in popularity, in spite of her efforts to keep it filled with wax likenesses of people prominent in the public eye. Now she had two sons to support, born in 1798 and 1800, as well as her mother who still kept house for them.

It was in these uncertain circumstances that a new opportunity presented itself. A showman friend of her late 'uncle' Curtius, who was proprietor of an entertainment known as the Phantasmagoria, a kind of magic lantern show, suggested that she join him in partnership, taking a selection of her wax figures to join his presentation in the Lyceum Theatre in London. He assured her that, although there were already exhibitions of wax figures in England, there was nothing to compare in artistry and style with the *Salon de Cire*. Finally, in the autumn of 1802, she signed a partnership contract with the showman Philipstal. She had never been out of France and her only contact with English people had been with the visitors who came into the exhibition which had always attracted tourists. Her decision, however, did not seem rash or imprudent, and Philipstal owed a debt of gratitude. In 1793 at the height of the Revolution, Philipstal, during his magic-lantern-type show, very popular in Paris, had inadvertently shown a likeness of the guillotined King Louis XVI, an error which had landed him in prison and in danger of losing his own head. He had been saved by Curtius's relationship with the powerful Robespierre, who had accepted a bribe, and had the unhappy Philipstal released.

Philipstal was German-born and, in spite of the hostilities between France and England, had been able to take his Phantasmagoria to London for the first time in 1801. He booked the Lyceum Theatre in the Strand for his enterprise. In October he advertised the opening of his 'Grand Cabinet of Optical and Mechanical Curiosities'. This exhibition was in three parts, firstly Automata and other mechanical devices, followed by Optical Illusion, 'different spectres, ghosts, or spirits of departed persons'. The finale was a superb 'Mechanical-Optical Firework'. Marie was, of course, familiar with Philipstal's show. Curtius had always been interested in optics and lighting, and had experimented with lighting effects in the *Salon de Cire*. She too paid special attention to the lighting of the exhibition.

Philipstal's Phantasmagoria was something of a novelty in London.

Apart from regular times of showing he advertised that the 'nobility and gentry' could have a special performance presented at any time of the day provided prior notice was given. The show proved popular and profitable. It ran through November into December, when Philipstal announced in the press that he was having the seating arrangement of boxes removed to make more space.

The Phantasmagoria was still attracting good audiences in January 1802, and in February Philipstal informed the public that he had obtained royal letters patent for his entertainment, an achievement which was recorded in the widely-read periodical, the *Annual Register*.

The Lyceum Theatre at this time was in fact two theatres, the Upper Theatre and the Lower Theatre. Philipstal made his presentation on the upper level, while the lower theatre was occupied by 'Egyptiana'. This was of interest to Marie, as Curtius had acquired an Egyptian mummy many years earlier, which she still kept on show. Philipstal evidently had some connection with this Egyptian exhibition, for in March, while still running his Phantasmagoria upstairs, he announced that he had extended the attraction on the lower level 'into the regions of Spectography'. Philipstal then left the Lyceum Theatre probably for a short visit to Paris, but he was back there in June, and in July added 'The Sorcerer's Anniversary' to his show. He remained there till August when he returned to France and was replaced at the Lyceum by a Mr Charles with his 'Auricular Communications of an Invisible Girl'. This Mr Charles would play a part in Madame Tussaud's life two years later.

When Philipstal got back to Paris after his successful London enterprise and with enviably full pockets, the political scene had changed. England and France were no longer at war. Prime Minister Pitt, who had refused to negotiate with Revolutionary France unless the Bourbons were returned to the throne had been replaced by Prime Minister Addington. England no longer had allies, and the country desired peace. In France Napoleon Bonaparte was First Consul (Marie had modelled him from life, and his figure stood triumphant in her exhibition). Bonaparte realised the maritime supremacy of England and wanted a breathing space. In March 1802 the Treaty of Amiens was signed. There were no longer any bars to English and French citizens visiting each other's countries. If Madame Tussaud wanted to restore her waning fortunes and take the still famous *Salon de Cire* to London she could do so. Philipstal was eager for partnership. There were advantages on both sides. The artistry of her wax figures would attract extra visitors and, although ten years had passed since the execution of Louis XVI, the English were still deeply interested in the fate of the Bourbons and the terrors of the Revolution. For Marie it was an opportunity to break new ground in partnership with an experienced fellow-showman, already popular in London.

After some obstruction from the Commissioner of Police, Fouché, who was well aware that Marie had modelled the guillotined heads of the King and Queen and Revolutionary leaders – he said so skilled an artist should not leave France – she obtained the necessary passport and documents, and was able to sign a contract with Philipstal. Its terms were not favourable to her, but if she wished to go to London she was in no position to haggle. Once signed the contract was binding, and she could only buy herself out if she wished at any time to break with Philipstal.

The regulations with which Marie would have to comply on arrival seemed relatively simple. They had been considerably eased since the Peace of Amiens in March when the interchange of travellers between France and England became possible again. On disembarking, provided her documents were in order, an officer at the Customs House would provide her with a certificate giving personal particulars, profession, country of origin. Within a week of arrival this certificate had to be presented to the Chief Magistrate or another specified official of the city or township in which the alien was residing, and a copy of it was sent by the Customs House official to the office of His Majesty's Principal Secretaries of State. 'His Majesty' was King George III who had sat on the English throne for forty-two years.

The way was clear for Marie to start packing the wax figures most likely to appeal to her unknown English audience, and to take sad leave of her family. The direction of the *Salon de Cire* was entrusted to her husband François and the staff she had trained – it was after all, she thought, only for some months. Her mother would care for her two-year-old younger son, another François; Marie intended to take her elder son Joseph with her although he was only four. While her training in modelling in wax had started at the age of six, when Dr Curtius had noticed his housekeeper's daughter's precocious talent, Joseph's training had begun as soon as his fingers were strong enough to handle a ball of softened wax. He too was precocious and bright. Always at his mother's side, the wax exhibition, the studios, and the workrooms were his playground. Already he could perform little tasks, and Marie was determined that Joseph should be equipped to step into Curtius's shoes in due course. Also he would be a comfort during the lonely times she would experience while on foreign soil.

The packing of more than thirty wax heads, and the bodies of stuffed and moulded leather with carved wooden arms and legs where they were hidden by clothing, was a lengthy and delicate task. The heads included the guillotined heads of the King and Queen of France and the Revolutionaries Robespiere, Fouquier-Tinville, Carrier, and Hébert. The tableau of Marat stabbed in his bath must go too. Voltaire and Benjamin Franklin would appeal to English audiences, and there was beautiful young Madame du Barry, modelled by Curtius when she was twenty-two. With Napoleon Bonaparte, modelled from life when he became First Consul, the collection would span the course of the French Revolution. Materials for modelling and repair had to be packed as well, but finally all was finished, and late in October 1802 Madame Tussaud set forth with her son Joseph and her wax exhibition to cross the English Channel. She did not know that she would never set foot in France again.

CHAPTER I

The Lyceum Theatre

———————◆———————

N O records have survived of Madame Tussaud's experiences during her arduous journey from Paris to a Channel port, but she and her crated exhibition arrived safely in London at the beginning of November 1802.

Fortunately there had been no trouble with Customs officers prying into the carefully labelled packing cases. Indeed they seem to have been generally quite lax in the performance of their duties now England and France were no longer at war. The famous novelist Fanny Burney, who travelled to France with her French émigré husband soon after the Peace of Amiens, noted in her diary how casual Customs officials had been at both the English and French Channel ports.

Arrived in London Marie lodged in Surrey Street, which was convenient for the Lyceum Theatre, located in Wellington Street across the Strand. It was also only a short distance from a royal residence known as 'The Queen's House' (now Buckingham Palace). This was the favourite home of King George III and Queen Charlotte. A mansion originally built by the Duke of Buckingham, the King had bought it in 1762 and it was settled on Queen Charlotte in 1775. All the royal children apart from the Prince of Wales had been born there.

In what scant spare time she had Marie could take Joseph to the gates to watch the comings and goings of the Royal Household, and perhaps even get a sight of the King and Queen themselves. It was a homely place, very different from the vast and splendid palace of Versailles where she had lived during those pre-Revolutionary years when she worked as art tutor to Madame Elizabeth, King Louis XVI's sister, and mingled daily with royalty. At least Marie was in the vicinity of a King and Queen again, and perhaps one day there might be a chance of closer contact.

Without delay she set about unpacking and setting up the exhibition in the Lower Theatre of the Lyceum while Philipstal occupied the Upper Theatre. Marie knew that in quality and style she must excel if she were to achieve the much-needed success she sought in this foreign country. Philipstal's Phantasmagoria might have the advantage of novelty, but wax portraiture had a very long history in England and some of her predecessors had been well-known as artists and exhibitors.

The sculpting of likenesses in wax had begun several centuries earlier with the creation of funeral effigies to be carried on the coffins of royal or eminent personages. The earliest of these was probably the effigy of King Henry III who died in 1272, and the last that of the beautiful Duchess of Buckingham, deceased in 1745. Other forms of wax portraiture were also practised.

Abraham Simon was one of the earliest artists in wax specialising in 'miniature' portraits modelled in relief. He had been medallist to the great Queen Christina of Sweden and came to England about 1642. Among the portraits he modelled were those of King Charles II, and Henry Cromwell, fourth son of Protector Oliver Cromwell and one-time Lord Deputy of Ireland, who, after the Restoration, retired to live peacefully in Cambridgeshire.

In 1684 a famous French wax modeller, Antoine Benoist, came to England specially to model wax busts of King James II and members of his Court. He set a standard of workmanship that was a criterion of excellence for later sculptors in wax. Among these, and a contemporary of Madame Tussaud, was Samuel Percy who died in 1820. Many of his 'miniature' portraits were in high relief, and he made skilful use of coloured waxes.

There were two celebrated female wax modellers working in the latter part of the eighteenth century. The eccentric Patience Wright who, like Marie, had modelled Benjamin Franklin's head when in Paris, worked mostly in London from 1772 until her death in 1786. Her life-size portrait of the Earl of Chatham is still to be seen in Westminster Abbey. Patience was possibly the most fashionable artist in wax of her day and moved in high society. Like many contemporaries she enjoyed a practical joke. Horace Walpole recounted that when Lady Aylesbury was visiting Mrs Wright's house she addressed a word to what she thought was a housemaid who failed to reply and on closer inspection turned out to be a wax figure.

Catherine Andras was equally fashionable as a portraitist in wax. Fourteen years younger than Marie she first exhibited in the Royal Academy in 1799 and continued to do so until 1824. Catherine received an award for a portrait of Princess Charlotte, and her full-size figure of Nelson (now in Westminster Abbey) caused a sensation with its uncanny resemblance to the living Admiral. In 1801, the year before Marie arrived in London, Catherine Andras was appointed 'Modeller in Wax' to Queen Charlotte.

However, neither of these woman artists was ever connected with an exhibition shown for public entertainment. In this field too Marie's predecessors dated back at least to the middle of the seventeenth century. A broadsheet of 1647, *The Dagonizing of Bartholomew Fair*, mentions 'wonders made of wax' on show at the famous fair in Smithfield. There is an entry in the Lord Mayor of London's Waiting Book of 1685 noting that permission was given to one Jacob Schalek to show his waxworks in the City of London.

In 1696 a Mrs Mills, 'the greatest Artist in Europe', was exhibiting full-sized wax figures in premises in Durham's Yard off the Strand. She advertised in the *Postman* of February that year. Her 'excellent figures' included those of King Charles II, King William and Queen Mary of Blessed Memory, and Oliver Cromwell 'in full stature, the Muscles, Sinews, and Veins appearing all over his body so that you would take it for life itself did it not want motion'.

Among Mrs Mills's competitors were Mr and Mrs Goldsmith. He advertised his exhibition in Green Court, Old Jewry, in the *Postman* of August 1697. As well as a portrait of the late Queen Mary 'curiously done in wax', a tableau of 'several Persons of Quality with a Fine Banquet' was a special attraction. Mrs Goldsmith had a mention in the *Daily Courant* of 6 August 1703, which announced, 'On Wednesday last, Mrs Goldsmith, the famous woman for waxwork, brought to Westminster Abbey the effigy of that celebrated beauty the Duchess of Richmond said to be the richest figure ever set up in King Henry's Chapel.'

The most famous of Marie's predecessors was undoubtedly the extraordinary Mrs Salmon, who modelled and exhibited her figures from the early years of the eighteenth century. Her premises were located in what is now St Martin's le Strand in the City. She was advertising in the *Tatler* in 1710 and Addison wrote about her in the *Spectator* in 1711.

Mrs Salmon's exhibition comprised some one hundred and forty figures 'as big as life'. In her handbills she drew attention to her 'moving waxworks', so some were evidently animated by a form of clockwork. Later she moved the exhibition to a house on the north side of Fleet Street near The Horn tavern. She said there was more room there for the carriages of the gentry which blocked St Martin's le Grand.

Mrs Salmon's death at the age of ninety was announced in March 1760. In her latter years, still active, she was obsessed with death and said to decorate her bonnets with coffin trimmings and sleep with a pall as coverlet.

On Mrs Salmon's demise her exhibition was purchased by a Mr Clark, variously described as a surgeon and a solicitor who lived nearby in Chancery Lane. His wife took over the management retaining the trade name and the sign of the Golden Salmon. However in 1794 the premises were purchased by a banking concern. Mrs Clark had to move across Fleet Street into what is now known as Prince Henry's Room, over an archway leading into the Temple. She was still established there when Marie arrived in London, but did not really present any competition, for the exhibition had sadly declined since Mrs Salmon's heyday. Its main attraction was a wax figure near the entrance which kicked out at visitors as they came in. But Mrs Clark continued the exhibition until 1812. Her wax exhibition was sold for £500 and moved to Water Lane where it languished for another decade before being broken up.

There was also a Mrs Bullock who might have been considered more of a competitor. Her 'Beautiful Cabinet of Wax Figures' contained portraits 'all the full size of life, striking likenesses of the Persons they represent and dressed in the most fashionable and splendid manner of their respective countries'. None, however, had Madame Tussaud's range of French Royal and Revolutionary portraits, nor her years of training in presentation and lighting, and the flair she had acquired from her 'uncle' Curtius. She had the disadvantage of speaking no English. While four-year-old Joseph learned quickly, Marie was fortunate in finding a reliable interpreter, a Swiss who her husband François had once met.

Already there was friction arising between Marie and Philipstal. During her three months stay at the Lyceum Theatre he advertised his own Phantasmagoria but did not give her any publicity in the press. He only mentioned an Egyptian mummy on display in the Lower Theatre. This mummy certainly attracted visitors downstairs to the area where her skilfully grouped and lit wax figures were set out, and it remained a feature of the exhibition for many years to come, often mentioned in handbills and advertisements. She may have brought it with her from Paris, one of the many curios that gave added interest to the *Salon de Cire* in the Boulevard du Temple, or it may have originated at the earlier exhibition of Egyptiana in the Lower Theatre on Philipstal's previous visit.

Although deprived of direct publicity, Marie's collection soon attracted distinguished visitors, eager to look at the French Royal family and the 'monsters' of the Revolution. Almost immediately she was able to start modelling portraits of English men and women who were in the contemporary public eye.

One of the first of these sitters was Sir Francis Burdett. It is possible that Marie may already have met Sir Francis as a young man at her 'uncle's table. When his education was finished he had toured Switzerland and France and resided in Paris during the early years of the Revolution. Already liberal-minded he had attended debates in the National Assembly and visited many of the political clubs, such as the Jacobin Club of which Curtius was an early member. The young man would certainly have visited the famous *Salon de Cire* in the Boulevard du Temple at some time during his stay.

On his return to England in 1793 Sir Francis made a wealthy marriage with Sophia Coutts, daughter of the prominent banker. Enthused with the liberal ideas he had imbibed in France, Sir Francis entered Parliament as member for Newcastle in 1796, and soon made a name for himself as a strong supporter of parliamentary electoral reform, free speech, and opposition to war with France. Such war, he claimed, was but a futile effort to stifle the flame of Liberty. He exposed various popular grievances and investigated conditions and abuses in the prisons.

By 1802, when Marie moulded his likeness, Sir Francis had become a prominent political figure. He stood as Parliamentary candidate for Westminster in opposition to a magistrate who objected to the prison investigations he had instigated. Sir Francis won the seat by a large majority, but for two years a legal wrangle ensued as his opponents tried to nullify the electoral return. It was in this situation, while Sir Francis was the successful but disputed member for Westminster, that Marie added his portrait to the exhibition.

She was also able to model another man in the public eye in very different circumstances. He was Colonel Edward Despard the conspirator. An Irishman, he had entered the British Army at the age of fifteen and served until 1790 when he was recalled from the West Indies to face some charges that proved unfounded. His demands for compensation finally earned him two years in prison. On his release he became involved with six associates in a crack-brained plot to assassinate King George III and seize the Tower and the Bank of England. This was quickly discovered. Despard and his fellows were arrested early in November 1802, soon after Marie's arrival in London. On 21 February 1803 the now notorious Colonel Despard was pulled on a hurdle to the place of execution, hanged, drawn and quartered.

Colonel Despard's remains were handed over to his family for burial. Marie performed a familiar task, whether due to her own initiative or at the request of relatives is not known. She took a mould from the wretched Colonel Despard's decapitated head. The resulting likeness proved that the English too had a taste for horror. It remained in the exhibition until 1819 and was the first of many heads of notorious convicted criminals, 'modelled from the face after death' as the catalogues put it, in what would years later become known as the Chamber of Horrors.

During the months at the Lyceum Theatre Marie also had the immense gratification of her first royal sitter in England, in the person of the Duchess of York. The Duchess was the wife of King George III's second son Frederick Augustus. Born Princess Frederica Charlotte Ulrica Catherine, the daughter of Frederick William II of Prussia, she married the soldier Duke in 1791. The marriage was not happy and the couple soon separated. The Duchess retired to the country seat of Oaklands. Having no children she occupied herself mainly with her pet dogs.

Honouring the exhibition with a visit – Marie was well accustomed to receiving royalty – the childless Duchess asked Marie to model a sleeping child for her. She gave permission for a replica to be shown in the exhibition where it remained for many years, and she allowed Marie to use her name as patron in future handbills, posters, and catalogues.

Some years later the Duke of York had to resign his post as Commander-in-Chief, on account of scandal about trafficking in appointments by his mistress Mary Ann Clarke. Marie modelled her likeness too.

While at the Lyceum Marie's relations with her partner Philipstal worsened. She now realised how unsatisfactory were the financial arrangements she had made. Philipstal could claim half her takings, which were much larger than those of the Phantasmagoria although he had not given her any publicity, while he refused to make any contribution to the running expenses of the wax exhibition. Her purse was not filling at the rate it should under this unfair agreement. Philipstal was showing signs of jealousy at her success too. Would she do better to return to France at the end of the Lyceum season? Back to her husband and family and little son, and the familiar surroundings of the Boulevard du Temple? But Marie had worked hard in London. She had established her exhibition as an entertainment of quality, she had obtained a Royal patron, had modelled distinguished English personalities, and above all gained personal status and repute as one who had mingled with the Royal family and Court of France. She now had to decide whether these factors outweighed her personal distress at distancing herself even further from the three-year-old François and the rest of her family as well as the anxieties and risks of packing up and transporting the exhibition on such a long journey to the north.

CHAPTER II

Scotland 1803/4

AT the beginning of April 1803 Philipstal advertised the impending closure of his Phantasmagoria at the Lyceum Theatre. He proposed going to Edinburgh and presenting his show to a new Scottish public. The wax exhibition would come too, though the strains between Marie and himself were now considerable. Letters that she wrote to her husband and family at this period survive and trace the growing hostility between them. On 25 April 1803 she wrote to husband François: 'He is angry. Philipstal treats me as you do. He has left me all alone.' Nonetheless Marie agreed to make the Scottish tour.

Short of breaking her contract and returning to Paris she had little choice. She could not stay longer in the Lower Theatre of the Lyceum and, according to tradition, was eager to leave the place. She was always extremely alert to the danger of fire, and learned that the inventor Winsor was about to demonstrate his new system of gas lighting in the upper part. She feared the risk of a conflagration. Winsor had arranged to give a series of lectures and to demonstrate his method of conveying the gas from room to room and his mode of lighting by gas chandeliers. There were several reasons too why Marie considered that a Scottish tour could prove a profitable proposition compared with possible visits to provincial towns (which in later years she would tour regularly).

In early 1803 it was obvious from the political relations of England and France that hostilities would break out again. Severe restrictions on the movement of aliens would then be imposed, the position of a lone Frenchwoman on the move could become difficult indeed. Scotland was sufficiently distant to offer a measure of security and there were plenty of French people there. Since 1802 the Comte d'Artois, younger brother of the late King Louis XVI of France, had made his headquarters in exile at Holyrood Palace in Edinburgh, and resided there almost continuously. Edinburgh was a favourite refuge for expatriate French, and Marie could be certain of finding friendly compatriots.

As regards Edinburgh itself, the city had been developing over a forty year period. It had undergone extensive rebuilding which was virtually completed with the opening of elegant Charlotte Square in 1800. Edinburgh had had a theatre since 1769, and by the early nineteenth century claimed to have more native talent than any other city in the country except London. It was a good venue for appreciative audiences.

Social life there was active and colourful while literature and the arts flourished. The standard of living was high and new uses of leisure went hand in hand with increased domestic comfort. Old inconveniences had disappeared, such as the 'water caddies' who used to carry water round to householders. Newly piped water was now in extensive supply.

In the world of entertainment public functions and theatre performances were freely patronised for, with the dominance of the moderate party in the Church of Scotland, old Puritan influences had diminished. Fashions too had greatly changed. Scottish ladies had abandoned brocade and powdered hair for new French classical styling in flimsy muslins and gauzes. This mode had reached its apex in Paris about 1800 when French women discarded their stays and petticoats completely in favour of nothing but flesh-coloured tights under their diaphanous dresses, though in England and Scotland the fashions remained more discreet, with puff sleeves, ribbon sashes under the bust, and lace-trimmed fichus.

Circumstances for touring in Scotland seemed favourable. The rapidly growing population had more money to spend than had ever been the case before. In the early nineteenth century the first phase of the Industrial Revolution, with the setting up of Scottish wool, linen, and cotton industries, was putting good money into more people's pockets. They were more mobile too for Scottish roads were rapidly improving. In 1801 a Commission for Highland Roads and Bridges had been set up under the famous engineer Thomas Telford, and by 1803 many formerly isolated places were linked with stage coach services.

In view of all these favourable conditions, and despite the fact that she was alone and at odds with her partner Philipstal, Marie could face the prospect of the hazardous journey to Scotland in reasonably good heart. She was, in fact, glad that she would start single-handed, for Philipstal proposed to delay his own departure for a short while, in order to discuss business with a gentleman Marie referred to as 'The Baron'.

Marie herself had business to do before she left London. She visited a lawyer called Wright, who had offices near Manchester Square and she signed a power of attorney giving her husband François control over all her property in Paris and enabling him to raise money on it. The document survives today. There is no evidence at this point that Marie had decided to abandon her family and native land for good, though she wrote to François that she intended to keep the promise made before she left – that she would not return without 'a full purse'. The fact that her husband evidently wished to borrow money must have steeled her resolution.

When she had packed everything and was ready to leave London, Marie had her most serious dispute yet with Philipstal. He refused to hand over any money for current expenses, saying he had already paid for the sea voyage to Edinburgh. Marie retorted with the threat of immediately returning to Paris with her ready-packed exhibition. This induced Philipstal to part with the sum of £10. She was making the voyage by sailing ship (the first steamship was not built until four years later). The sea did not prove friendly. She and Joseph, with the considerable number of packing cases, left London on 27 April and the ship did not reach Edinburgh till 10 May. On the day after her arrival Marie wrote to her husband and family describing the perils of the voyage and the trials that awaited her on arrival.

'Dozens of confident people were ill through the bad weather. The sea was terribly rough. We saw three storms which lasted three days and everyone had to go below. The boat rolled in a terrifying manner and the Captain who had made this voyage a hundred times had never seen one like it. Nini (her pet name for Joseph) was not afraid. He made friends with the Captain and with everybody . . . he wanted to train Nini to be a sailor and said he would be a tribute to France . . . everybody called him "little Bonaparte".'

Marie herself complained of feeling the motion of the ship for several days after arrival, but at the time she had to forget her malaise and cope with unforeseen difficulties. It turned out that Philipstal had not paid for the carriage of the crates, as he told Marie he would when he grudgingly handed her £10 for travelling expenses. The Captain refused to unload the crates until he had his money. 'If I had not found Monsieur Charles we should have been obliged to let everything go. Monsieur Charles lent me £30 to pay for everything, of which we had to pay £18 for the wax figures on the voyage.' It was indeed a fortunate chance that this acquaintance was presenting his ventriloquist show *The Invisible Girl* in Edinburgh. He had visited Paris with this presentation, and had followed on after Philipstal on his earlier enterprise at the Lyceum Theatre. He admired Marie and her artistry, and proved a good friend in this moment of crisis.

Marie's fortunes changed with her arrival in Edinburgh. She was rid, if only temporarily, of Philipstal. She was quickly able to find a large, suitably decorated and furnished room in which to mount her exhibition, and comfortable lodgings for herself and Joseph. Her landlady spoke good French and, through a recommendation of 'the Baron' with whom Philipstal was concluding his business in London, she obtained the services of a competent interpreter, 'a very worthy man' who spoke French, German and English.

Marie was much taken with Edinburgh, which she described to her husband as a lovely little town and from where she could see mountains with snow still on them. In Edinburgh Castle she found some compatriots and also 'a lady-in-waiting' who had spent most of her life in France.

This new friend was more likely to have been the wife of some official at the Castle, as the Governor at the time was unmarried. The lady was a congenial companion, and Marie spent as much time as she could with her, feeling, as she remarked, almost as if she were back in Paris. Joseph was dressed 'like a little Prince' and there were some French boys at the Castle with whom he played.

The friendship and patronage of these new friends up at the Castle gave Marie the prestige she so desired for herself as well as her exhibition. 'I am taken for a great lady,' she told her family. 'I am liked in this town as much as in my own country and not treated as a foreigner.' But in spite of her comfortable lodgings at 28 Thistle Street and her new friends, Marie was lonely and homesick. François was a dilatory correspondent, and she begged him to answer her letters more quickly, to remember her to her mother and aunt and, above all, to her three-year-old son from whom she was so far away.

Marie opened her Salon on 18 May at three o'clock in the afternoon. In Philipstal's absence she could handle her own promotion and publicity, and the public responded. 'It's all very satisfactory for the Salon,' she wrote, 'and I hope to make money here in this city. Everybody is amazed at my figures.' Joseph helped to the best of his ability: 'He is a very hard worker and keeps his head down – sometimes we are too tired for supper. We have promised ourselves a trip to the country on Sunday to try to get some wild honey, to pass the day in the country which is very pretty and with the kindest people.'

When Philipstal finally arrived in Edinburgh he was jealous of her success, and their relations remained hostile. Marie was happy that there was no room for the Phantasmagoria in Bernard's Rooms where she was enjoying her success, and he had to find another location in the Corri Rooms. In spite of this she still had to hand over half her receipts to Philipstal, and out of her remaining half buy her own materials and meet her own expenses. Supported by the helpful Monsieur Charles and the new friends she had made in Edinburgh, Marie became the more determined to buy out Philipstal and work for herself as soon as she could.

She still had not ventured to use her own name, Madame Tussaud, on her handbills and posters. It was Curtius's name that people remembered when they had seen her 'uncle's' famous *Salon de Cire* in Paris, and she relied on it still. She advertised her collection of wax figures as 'accurate models from life in Composition from the Great Curtius of Paris'. It was a splendid assembly that met the eyes of visitors as they entered the spacious room in which the exhibition was arranged. It included the First Consul, Napoleon Bonaparte and Madame Bonaparte, the late Royal Family of France, Voltaire, Rousseau and Frederick the Great of Prussia. Benjamin Franklin was there too, and the recumbent figure of the beautiful Madame du Barry at the age of twenty-two, which Curtius had modelled before she became the King of France's mistress (still in the exhibition today as the *Sleeping Beauty*). 'Nothing like them has been seen in this city,' she wrote home triumphantly. Little Joseph, always at her side in the exhibition was also gratifyingly popular – 'the town is full of Nini' – and a portrait she modelled of the child was hailed as an excellent likeness.

Relations with her partner were not improved when Philipstal's show at the Corri Rooms, which opened on the evening of 15 June 1803, was unfortunately a complete disaster. He had brought a collection of automata as well as the usual magic-lantern type Phantasmagoria which he publicised as 'original, astounding and unparalleled experiments in the Science of Optics of which he is the sole inventor, and which were brought out of his native country Germany to do away with the belief in ghosts'. Alas, on the opening evening, his apparatus broke down and 'failed of producing the effect intended'. Philipstal was obliged to advertise his apologies and promise that the entertainment would proceed smoothly in future. Even so the Phantasmagoria and the automata did not attract the public as Marie's exhibition was doing.

In fact, she wrote to her family in the Boulevard du Temple, while everyone regarded her as a great lady, Philipstal with his Phantasmagoria was considered a charlatan. Her desire to separate from her partner increased: 'For a long time I have done everything myself without Monsieur Philipstal,' she said.

The wax exhibition in Bernard's Rooms was open from eleven o'clock in the morning till four in the afternoon, and again from six till eight in the evening. The admission charge was 2/- and she was getting as many as one hundred and fifty visitors a day. The place was always busy, and she and Joseph had little leisure. Her friend, Mr Charles, suggested partnership if she could extricate herself from her contract with Philipstal but Marie dismissed the idea at once. Mr Charles's *Invisible Girl* had been successful too in Edinburgh, but Marie wrote to her husband: 'Once bitten by Philipstal I do not want any more joint enterprises, no matter with whom. I have had a very unhappy experience, and consider I am better off on my own.' It was a principle she stuck to all her life. Her only partners were her sons.

Though François had written suggesting she return to Paris this was something she was not prepared to do. She had not yet achieved her 'well-filled purse', and was surprised her husband should expect her to leave before she had cleared up her affairs with Philipstal. It would have been very difficult anyway. The Peace of Amiens had broken down in May, the ports were closed and communication between Britain and France severed. In Edinburgh Marie felt safe with so many compatriots and friends around her. She urged her dilatory husband to work hard in her absence, and look after her mother and the rest of the family, particularly her second son, now three years old.

By the end of July she had straightened out her affairs with Philipstal, not without bitter disputes since Marie had no means of checking the accounts he presented to her. She handed over to him £150, his share of her receipts, and parted with another hundred pounds to reduce her debt to him on account of money he advanced at the start of their partnership. Urged on by Mr Charles, who was still hoping they might join forces, she consulted Scottish lawyers but they advised there was no way of breaking the contract without his consent, even though its terms were entirely in his favour. Philipstal refused to consider separation.

Edinburgh had been full of visitors for the Summer Horse Show, but now Marie's receipts began to falter. She was disappointed, but reduced her entrance fee to 1/-, describing herself as a woman 'bowed down with fear and anxiety'. But she and Joseph remained in good health and she took great pleasure in the progress of her son, who was now taking English lessons and had learned to read.

At the beginning of October 1803 Marie moved her exhibition to Glasgow. Philipstal had already visited the town, but she was able to go on her own. It was a successful venture. The first receipts of £40 more than covered the cost of the move. How much Marie regretted that she had not been able to pay Philipstal off in Edinburgh. She had not seen him for some time now, but was still bound to him.

Apart from this worry everything was going well. Joseph had quickly become fluent in English and could act as interpreter even though he was only five years old. She was distressed, though, that there had been no letter from her husband for three months. Of course communication between France and England was now difficult, but her letters seemed to get through. 'Is it possible,' she wrote reproachfully, 'that you have forgotten me?' and hoped that it was possible for him to take on the duties of head of the family.

Marie and Joseph lodged very comfortably in Glasgow with Mr Colin, a pastry cook, in Wilson Street and the exhibition was satisfactorily set up in the New Assembly Rooms in Ingram Street. Mr Colin was a most respectable man who had already resided at Wilson Street since 1790 and was to become a Guild Brother and a Burgess of Glasgow.

The exhibition was well located in the New Assembly Rooms. For the first time Marie was able to have two Salons. The second, a harbinger of the Chamber of Horrors and referred to as the Separate Room, contained the guillotined death heads of Robespierre, Fouquier-Tinville, Hébert and Carrier as well as the full-sized Tableau of Marat lying assassinated in his bath. There was a scale model of the guillotine and two models of the Bastille showing the once dreaded Paris fortress before and after its capture and subsequent demolition by the Revolutionary mobs in July 1789. The Egyptian mummy that Philipstal had advertised at the Lyceum theatre was there too, and the bloodstained shirt worn by Henry IV of France when he was assassinated in 1610. This had been one of the relics acquired by Curtius for the *Salon de Cire* which Marie had brought with her. Marie advertised in the *Glasgow Herald and Advertiser*. She offered to model portraits too 'in the fullest imitation of life' and added: 'The artist can also model from the dead body as well as from animated nature.' She still did not promote her own name, merely referring to herself as 'the artist'.

The exhibition did well in Glasgow throughout the autumn, but in December receipts began to fall. Marie planned to move to Greenock. She had taken £250 during her season in Glasgow, satisfactory but not so good as Edinburgh. 'We will exhibit in some Scottish towns, and there are some fairly large ones, and the time will be spent in a country of peace and quiet.'

Philipstal, however, had other plans. He was now in Dublin, accompanied by his colleague 'the Baron' and their servants. Marie heard of his arrival in December and wrote: 'I can breathe much more freely now that Monsieur Philipstal is a long way away and everything can only improve.' Philipstal intended that she should join him there in Dublin but for the moment she refused: 'At least it will not be this winter [1803/4] and during this bad weather at that. I will not go there until I am sure that there is no danger for the exhibition and myself and when peace comes to that country.'

Marie had lost none of the political awareness instilled into her from an early age by the politically-minded Curtius. She knew enough of the troubles in Ireland to make her wish to stay away. The Society of United Irishmen, founded by Wolfe Toone, wanted to gain independence for Ireland by revolutionary means, and appealed for French aid. In 1796 France had sent 15,000 troops under the command of General Hoche (whose portrait had been in the *Salon de Cire* in the Boulevard du Temple). Gales had dispersed the fleet carrying them and the effort came to nothing. A year later a second large-scale French military expedition was abandoned.

The Irish Rebellion was over and defeated before Marie left Paris but she knew sporadic conflict continued. She had no wish to find herself again in a country seeking liberation by revolution. It was wiser to remain in Scotland, with England and France renewing hostilities and Napoleon planning invasion.

In January 1804 she left for Greenock to open her exhibition there. She was happy to be free of Philipstal but was still periodically overcome with homesickness. She sent a forwarding address, via an Edinburgh friend, hopeful of more frequent letters from her husband, and exhorted him: 'Embrace all my dear family, my dear François, my dear mother and my dear aunt for Nini [Joseph] and I. My friend, I hope it will not be long before I am with you again. I live for that happy moment. I am tormented by not seeing you.' But she ended on a practical note: 'Let me know if you are getting any work.'

Marie's intention of touring Scotland till the spring brought better weather conditions was quickly quashed by Philipstal, who demanded her departure for Ireland as soon as her Greenock season ended. Under the terms of her contract with him she had to obey – till she could buy him out. Her venture across the Channel had done well financially, and she had gained confidence during her weeks alone in Glasgow, free of the constant altercations. She could not have known, as she and Joseph once again dismantled the exhibition in Greenock, that she would remain four years in Ireland and would shortly take a decision that would change the course of her life.

CHAPTER III

The Irish Years 1804/8

THE Ireland to which Marie Tussaud sailed early in February 1804 was not a peaceful place. Although active rebellion and French attempts at invasion had subsided, the Act of Union with England, passed in 1801, was bitterly opposed by many. The Irish statesman and orator Henry Grattan was one of those most fiercely against it. Before long Marie would be modelling his portrait.

The 'Annual Register' for 1804 records that there were still periodic movements of rebellion amongst the disaffected and there was often cause for anxiety and alarm. The Catholics were pressing their demand for equal rights, but King George III refused to consider Catholic Emancipation. From 1801 martial law had generally prevailed throughout the country and there were continual rumours of secret missionaries sent in by Napoleon Bonaparte and threats of further attempts at a French invasion.

However this kind of atmosphere was one to which Marie was well accustomed – had she not survived the French Revolution? Apart from all the political unrest the circumstances did in fact seem very favourable for the presentation of her wax exhibition. Although there was distress amongst much of the population due to failing potato harvests and exhaustion after so much political agitation and uncertainty there was now a degree of comparative tranquillity, and the English garrisons established throughout the country had very limited opportunities for diversion and entertainment.

Of course there were restrictions and dangers. People were generally not allowed to be out after nine in the evening and persons of property felt they had little security. The Earl of Clinton said that when he was going out his servant brought him his gun as he brought him his hat. Nonetheless, both the native population and the occupying military were ready and willing to patronise entertainments when they could be found.

There were very considerable opportunities too for taking the exhibition on tour away from Dublin. In August 1803 there were nearly fourteen thousand military stationed in Ireland with infantry or cavalry regiments dispersed in more than twenty towns. The twenty-six regiments involved included The Queen's German Regiment. Troops were usually billeted in the towns as the Irish population was hostile to military under canvas, so accessibility to entertainment such as Madame Tussaud's wax exhibition was not a problem. Such countrywide garrisoning provided an almost captive audience, and one eager for some amusement. Pro-French feeling which was prevalent amongst some sections of the Irish people would also be helpful in securing the maximum number of visitors to gaze at the French portrait figures which were so important a feature of the show. The roads of Ireland were comparatively good too, as they were kept in repair by the various municipal authorities.

As Marie and six-year-old Joseph stood on deck watching the coast draw nearer, the aspect of this strange country must have heartened them. A contemporary publication, *Journal of a Tour in Ireland performed in 1804*, describes the beautiful view of Dublin Bay and the wooded countryside dotted with fine-looking gentlemen's residences. At one end of the bay was the fashionable resort of Blackrock and at the other smart hotels located by a pier with another building now converted into a barracks.

The elegant city of Dublin with its streets of gracious houses did, of course, have its darker side. The writer of this Journal noted: 'it is difficult to convey an idea of the vice, filth, and wretchedness in which the lower orders dwell and seem to delight.' Yet, even if luxuries were expensive, the necessaries of life were cheap and the people easygoing and light-hearted in their daily life.

Quite another picture, and one more important to Marie, was drawn by John Carr, whose *Stranger in Ireland* was published the year after her arrival. Carr speaks of the well paved and lighted (though dirty) streets. There was a strong literary life in the city and the ladies of Dublin society were 'handsome and finely formed'. They dressed with elegance and were frequently highly educated and vivacious in conversation. There were very few of these ladies who did not speak French, many of them 'with the purity of the native accent'. Their tables were furnished with an abundant style of cookery and order and good taste prevailed. There was a Museum at Trinity College which included anatomical specimens considered to be 'very beautiful'. Balls were held frequently in Dublin and other large towns. They were always well attended as there was such a paucity of other entertainment.

The sea was kinder on this voyage and the crates arrived without undue damage. Marie must have felt some apprehension when she saw the carts gathered on the quay awaiting their loads. A contemporary account describes the typical Dublin cart as a 'mere platform extending from shafts which hung on the horse's shoulders. The rear end was within a foot of the ground resting on the axle of two little wheels'. When heavily loaded the weight often overcame the strength of the horse which could even strangle itself in its efforts.

No advertisement or handbill of Marie's Dublin opening survives. She probably set up the exhibition in the Shakespeare Gallery in Exchequer Street, near fashionable Grafton Street. She had immediate success. With the figures skilfully grouped and lighted, people thronged in to gaze at her portraits of the famous and the infamous.

Receipts amounted to £100 a month and with her Scottish profits she managed to come to a financial arrangement to rid herself of 'that monster Philipstal'. It was a courageous decision. She also took another decision of which she informed her husband and family late in March. She was replying to a letter received from her husband which had taken five months to arrive, not entirely surprising seeing that England and France were at war and the ports closed. How long she had brooded over this decision we do not know, but she delivered the bombshell that she was not intending ever to return to her husband, the little son she missed so much, and her relatives, in a letter that started in an ordinary enough way:

A letter written to her husband from Waterford 20 June 1804, in which Marie Tussaud tells him 'now I work only for myself and my children'. *Madame Tussaud's archives.*

My dear friends, I have just received your letter of Sunday 27th October on 17th March. It made me very happy to know that you are all in good health. We are very well also and if only I had my darling François with me I could ask for nothing more. My son here no longer speaks a word of French. I can tell you that I have finished completely with M. Philipstal last February. God be thanked. Now I work for myself and my children and everything is going well. When I am in Dublin the takings can reach £100 sterling a month. People come in crowds every day from six o'clock till ten o'clock. My Cabinet is already well known with its portraits of famous and infamous men. I am very proud of it and I feel full of courage. My Cabinet is very much in demand and I have had a letter asking me to visit other towns so I leave for Cork which is about 100 miles to the South. I hope by working hard I can give my children a good start in life and that they may then turn out so that their father and mother can be proud of them. There will then be no cause to reproach me for doing them harm. This is the real wealth we can give them. I have no regrets.

Then, without pause, Marie states her future intentions with un-compromising bluntness:

The day I finished with M. Philipstal my enterprise became more important to me than returning to you. Adieu, adieu – we can each go our own way. Address your letters to the same place in Dublin and they will be forwarded. My compliments to all friends. We embrace you from the depths of our hearts a thousand times.
　　　　　I am for life
　　　　　Your wife Tussaud.

Marie Tussaud never set foot in France again, nor did she see her husband or her mother and other relatives again. Her second son, François, the beloved 'Françison', did not join his mother till he was twenty-one years old. What was the last straw that drove her to this drastic break can only be conjecture. She had already made over the Paris exhibition and her house property in Paris to her husband by giving him power of attorney before she left London. The Paris exhibition was already mortgaged. There could have been bad financial news in François Tussaud's letter of 27 October, or perhaps, exasperated by her husband's irresponsibility and having rid herself of her disastrous contract with Philipstal, Marie decided she wanted no more partners of any description. She could do better for herself and her children if she carried on alone, following her 'uncle' Curtius's principles and like him, devoting her life and energies to portraiture in wax.

For some time at least she continued to write as if nothing had happened. In early June she was showing in Waterford. She took the exhibition there by sea and endured another bad crossing and everybody was seasick except little Joseph, who appeared immune in the worst storms. 'Above everything else,' she wrote, 'we are rid of the monster Philipstal – God be thanked. Have no doubts that I shall do very well . . . I now work only for myself and my children. I am going to make money with my Salon.' Again she sends a thousand embraces, and, in spite of her earlier 'Adieux' for good, she finishes, 'And I am for life your wife Tussaud.'

When she wrote the last of her surviving letters sent to her husband, addressing it to 'Monsieur Tussaud, Maison Curtius, Boulevard du Temple', she was lodging at 16 Clarendon Street, Dublin. The voyage back to Dublin from Waterford had been yet another ordeal:

> We endured a terrible crossing. We struck a storm, and three vessels which had left port with us were sunk beside us in five minutes. You can well imagine my loss. I had to make good what I had lost . . . I hope to be quiet here and am just making some portraits of famous people in the town for my Salon which is drawing big crowds.

Among the famous people she modelled was Henry Grattan, a relentless opposer of the Act of Union and protagonist of Catholic emancipation.

The slack season – summer holidays – was approaching but the exhibition was still taking £6 or £7 a day, and expenses were not high. She was paying only twenty-five guineas for the hire of the room for six months. The winter season promised to be very profitable. Then they would travel. Plans for the spring of 1805, when road conditions would improve with better weather, included Cork, Limerick, and Belfast, each of which towns sheltered two regiments. The author of the *Journal of a Tour in Ireland* remarked on 'the very great multitude of troops crowded into every town we have passed' and considered Cork 'a beautiful town' with a handsome new bridge. Only a few of these Irish towns had a local press and for the publicity that Philipstal had denied her, Marie then relied on handbills and posters.

In Kilkenny, where the exhibition arrived in May 1805 *Finn's Leinster Journal* was the local newspaper, and she took the opportunity of advertising. Neither her own name nor that of Curtius (which was known in cosmopolitan circles but not in rural Ireland) was mentioned. The advertisement stated that the 'Grand European Cabinet of Figures' was open every day in the Grand Jury Room of the City Court House by permission of John Helsham Esq., Mayor, from eleven in the morning until dusk, opening on 21 May. Curtius's Cabinet in Paris had always included a number of curiosities, and Marie pursued the same policy. The Egyptian mummy was mentioned in the advertisement, but handbills gave more details. As an innovation in the way of a 'curiosity' there were tiny models of carriages, 'curiously formed in Gold, Ivory and Tortoiseshell, each of them attached to, and drawn by, a flea to the complete astonishment of the spectator'. Admission to the exhibition was one shilling and one penny including the flea-circus.

John Carr, writing in the year of Marie's visit described Kilkenny as a delightful little town whose annual theatricals attracted fashionable people from Dublin and around. There were also races, balls and concerts. It seems Marie's visit coincided with the theatricals which lasted about a month since she had to arrange her exhibition in the City Court House. During her touring years she preferred to show in a theatre, and the one in Kilkenny was reportedly small and elegant, laid out in boxes with a gallery at the back. Although her Kilkenny advertisements announced that 'her departure from here will be forever' thus drawing in visitors for a once-in-a-lifetime experience, Marie must have enjoyed this gay little place which was linked to the capital by the Dublin Mail coach.

However, bouts of homesickness still affected her. In her last surviving letter to her family she expresses doubts that her second son, now four years old, will recognise his mother or his brother Joseph, now 'a proud English gentleman since he really is English – as everybody believes him to be English as he speaks English so very well'. All Marie's pride and affection are centred on Joseph. She writes dotingly from her lodging in Clarendon Street, Dublin, of 'a child of great promise and of an intelligence without equal; everybody likes him'. To add to his accomplishments the six-year-old Joseph was now taking piano lessons from one of his mother's Dublin friends.

In November Marie paid another visit to Cork. Though not as sophisticated as Dublin, its society was refined and elegant and its houses handsome. John Carr's contemporary account speaks of Cork's 'superb barracks', and rich and picturesque prospects. The exhibition was set out in a spacious room in Mr Scragg's Hotel. Curfew restrictions were easier and in addition to daytime opening visitors were welcome between six and ten o'clock each evening. Here, in what was considered the second city of Ireland the *Cork Evening Post* advertised the 'Grand European Cabinet'. The admission price was quite high, two shillings and twopence. Marie stayed in Cork until Christmas 1805.

During the next two years of touring Ireland Marie made money and gained confidence in her own artistry and her powers of showmanship. The month of May 1808 found her in Belfast, with the exhibition open at No. 92 High Street. Here, advertising in the *Belfast News and Letters*, Marie Tussaud at last claims her rightful recognition.

MADAME TUSSAUD Artist of the Great European
CABINET OF PICTURES
Modelled from Life

In this advertisement, for the first time, she uses the term 'waxwork'. Hitherto her publicity had not explained the exact nature of the 'composition' used by the great Curtius for modelling his figures, although its resemblance to life was always stressed.

Marie remained in Belfast until June, when she took the decision to leave Ireland, where she had now been touring for four years, and return to Scotland. Peace had not come and there was no question of going back to London. The Napoleonic Wars were unabated. In that same June a small British army was ordered to sail from Cork to Portugal under Arthur Wellesley, later the Duke of Wellington. All the overseas possessions ceded to France under the Peace of Amiens would soon be reoccupied. Who could have imagined that several decades later the Duke of Wellington would frequently visit Madame Tussaud's exhibition in London, to gaze at her portrait of his old enemy Napoleon Bonaparte.

It was July 1808 when she once again saw her crates loaded on a ship bound for Greenock. This time there were no storms to create havoc and on 29 July the exhibition opened for a short stay in Greenock, in the Mason's Hall.

Marie never returned to Ireland. In 1821 she intended to be in Dublin for the State visit of the newly-crowned King George IV. This time complete shipwreck would stop her plans. But Marie's four years in Ireland had not been wasted ones. She had made money and established herself in her own right as an artist in wax and a skilful exhibitor. Now she was embarking on what would turn out to be no less than twenty-six years of gruelling travels the length and breadth of the land. Her establishment in London lay far ahead.

CHAPTER IV

Madame Tussaud's Travels

WHILE Marie set up her exhibition in Greenock her advertisements announced that she was on her way to London. In fact she did not reach the capital until 1809, and then only for a limited stay, the first of five visits before she settled there in 1835. No letters survive to indicate what led her to decide on a life of packing up, setting up and re-packing, always moving on. It was a daunting choice for a woman of forty-seven, who, prior to her arrival in London in 1802, had been brought up, lived, and worked in the heart of central Paris's show business area. Her itineraries can be traced through contemporary posters, handbills, local press articles, and mentions in diaries and memoirs of local people. All the while she maintained her image of superiority, an émigré from the French Revolution, and loyal to the Royal Family of France, though she had an admiration for Napoleon and his now discarded Empress Josephine who had been her patron in the post-Revolutionary days.

In all she visited seventy-five towns, and with the exception of a few large centres, such as London, Manchester, and Liverpool, only once or twice. She had experienced waning interest in the years before she left Paris, and was determined custom should nowhere make her exhibition seem stale in spite of the constant updating and additions. Her resolution not to return to Paris must have been steeled by the knowledge that she no longer owned the house and exhibition in the Boulevard du Temple, where her 'uncle' Curtius had built up his celebrity. In September 1808 it all passed into other hands on the foreclosure of a mortgage.

In April 1795 after the difficult months following Curtius's death in the previous autumn Marie, in her determination to keep the exhibition and its high standards going, had found herself obliged to borrow. She obtained a loan of 20,000 livres in assignats, the paper currency of the Revolution, from a Citizeness Salomé Reiss, who appears to have had some connection with the household as her name appears on documents connected with Curtius's death. In return Salomé Reiss would receive an annuity until such time as the debt was repaid.

François Tussaud evidently felt he could not, or did not wish to continue with this annuity. Possibly he also found the running of the exhibition burdensome and unprofitable without Marie's artistic skill and hard work to maintain its standards. Under the power of attorney over her French property, which Marie had signed before she left London for Scotland, he decided to cede No. 20 Boulevard du Temple and the exhibition to Salomé Reiss, including 'all the objects comprising the Salon of figures known as the Cabinet du Curtius. These objects include all the wax figures, all the costumes, all the moulds, all the mirrors, lustres, and glass. . . . Monsieur Tussaud herewith renounces any rights in this regard'. In return Madame Reiss renounced all rights to the annuity she had been receiving as interest on the original loan of 20,000 livres in assignats. Possibly she had not been receiving her annuity regularly since Marie's departure for England. François Tussaud may have needed the money himself as he had purchased a lease on the Théâtre des Troubadours. This was a building erected on a plot of ground owned by him in the Boulevard du Temple. The family moved from No. 20 to No. 52, one of the houses Curtius had purchased for letting which Marie had inherited from him. Her husband had no more dealings with wax portraiture or exhibitions, but concentrated on minor property deals, often connected with the theatre.

Whether or not Marie approved the abandonment of Curtius's life work we do not know. It was obviously in decline and though a wax exhibition continued on the site for a number of years it never achieved the celebrity nor the standards of artistry and presentation that Curtius had set and taught to his pupil Marie from the age of six. Had she wished to change her mind and return to her family she would have had to start from scratch to rebuild in the only art she knew.

Marie accepted the course on which she was now irrevocably set with composure, energy, a business-like turn of mind, and the increasingly useful help and support of her twelve-year-old son. She was a woman ahead of her time in independence of outlook and determination to maintain status and prestige even though entirely self-supporting, as few women of the period were. She saw her future way of life as the only means available to maintain personal independence. Marie never entered into any sort of partnership with a husband or colleague. Even her sons did not achieve full legal partnership until they were middle-aged men and circumstances made it necessary. François Tussaud and Philipstal had convinced her that she could do best for herself and her children by working alone and unsupported.

Though she was, of course, an alien – she never took English citizenship – travelling now held few hazards for Marie. While England and France were still at war she had established herself as a French Royalist, and was accepted as such. The battle of Trafalgar in 1805 had put an end to Napoleon's hopes of victory on the seas and invasion of England. Since 1807 ports on both sides of the Channel were under blockade. Marie now spoke enough English to conduct her business in it, and with the French Royalist image she had cultivated her nationality was more of an asset than a handicap. She was experienced now in the mechanics of touring, never staying in any place long enough for the novelty of the exhibition to wear thin. She traversed the land from Dumfries to Bristol, from Portsmouth to Yarmouth, often making short visits to smaller places where there was no local press and she had to depend on posters and handbills for publicity.

These years of travel were contemporary with the achievements of the great road-builders, Thomas Telford and John McAdam. When Marie began her journeyings in 1808 the going on the roads was very rough. A contemporary writer describes even the better routes as 'at once loose, rough and perishable, expensive, tedious and dangerous to travel on'. Over such surfaces she had to transport her fragile wax figures by horse and cart.

During the early nineteenth century Telford's system of road-building and McAdam's method of surfacing, known as 'macadamising' were increasingly used. Growing industrial development made a better road system essential, since the canals favoured by King George III and sea transport were no longer adequate for rapidly increasing trade. Even towards the end of her travelling years the railways were not sufficiently developed to serve her circuitous routes, though coaches 'flew' over the improved roads at more than ten miles an hour.

Marie and Joseph travelled with the carts and vans by hired coach, as surviving expense ledgers show. Unlike some of the show business folk who travelled the assize towns with their entertainments and had their own living vans, Marie and her son always took lodgings. A considerable number of closed carts or vans were required to transport the figures, with their stuffed leather bodies and carved wooden legs, and fragile wax heads and other areas of exposed flesh such as hands and arms, costumes, settings and props, moulds and material for mending and for new portraits. Marie seems to have been able to carry out her work in any surroundings. It is significant that in the inventory of Curtius's exhibition in the Boulevard du Temple, taken after his death in 1794, there is no indication of a separate professional studio. Materials for making the portraits were listed all over the building. At least towards the end of her travelling years, in the 1830s, Marie's vans were gaily decorated. There are ledger entries for the re-gilding of the 'caravans'.

There are other indications of the expenses of everyday life while touring. Marie had learned from Curtius the importance of lighting in the exhibition. Expenses for candles were always high. Food purchases and intermittent expenditure were listed. In 1810 the ledger of an Edinburgh watch repairer, James Ritchie & Son, clock-makers, records the collecting of Joseph's watch which had been left for repair and, in November, Madame Tussaud called in again to collect another watch. Joseph's gold watch was French and could once have belonged to Curtius, but the second watch had been bought from Robert Clench in Dublin.

In 1812 Marie left the house where she was lodging in Briggate, Leeds, to move to Manchester. The coach hire amounted to £1 4s. A Coventry local historian records that the exhibition was showing at St Mary's Hall, while Marie lodged at Hay Lane. This was in 1823, when Marie was sixty-two. She is described as 'an affable woman who told many queer tales of the French Revolution'. On this occasion she stayed at Coventry for about three weeks not only occupying St Mary's Hall, but also turning the Mayoress's Parlour into a 'chamber of horrors'.

An additional attraction for visitors was added to the exhibition of wax portraiture in 1814. This was the taking of silhouette portraits by means of 'a machine', and was first announced when the exhibition was in Bath. Marie must have been in an indulgent mood towards her sixteen-year-old, as the words 'Joseph Tussaud, Proprietor' appear both on poster and advertisement. Joseph operated the silhouette-making 'machine', and the finished silhouettes cost from 2s 0d to 5s 0d, Joseph continued this activity for thirteen years. He must have had dozens of sitters, but only one signed example of his silhouette portraiture is known.

The early nineteenth century was the age of elegant Assembly Rooms, and these were Marie's first choice of venue throughout her travelling years. The long pillared rooms gave the best opportunity for the brilliantly lit 'coup d'oeil' which met the visitor on entering, and is so often praised in contemporary local newspaper reports of the exhibition's visits. The number of full-length, splendidly and accurately dressed figures grouped in these rooms varied between seventy and ninety. Cramped space caused difficulties as Marie paid so much attention to the setting out and arrangement of figures and groups. In Norwich in 1819 she delayed her opening for a week as the number of figures, ninety, and the shortness of the daylight hours made arranging them to the best advantage a thorny problem. Even after the delay the results were not entirely successful. The *Norfolk Chronicle* reported that the figures were as well arranged as the size of the room – the large room at The Angel Inn – would admit, 'but certainly would have appeared to greater advantage in a larger space'.

If no Assembly Rooms or other large rooms of a similar type were available the next choice was a theatre, often to be found in larger towns such as Doncaster, Peterborough or Dover which were also visited by theatrical touring companies. Here problems of space were usually solved by boarding over the orchestra pit so that the necessary vista could be achieved.

No records exist as to where Marie showed in London when she reached it, but contemporary surviving catalogues state that her likenesses of King George III and Queen Charlotte were 'taken from life' in 1809. Whether the Royal couple submitted to the taking of life masks by Marie's skilled hands, or whether 'from life' was based on her sharp observance of Their Majesties in public cannot be certain. Marie had made some influential contacts during her stay at the Lyceum Theatre, though that was six years earlier, and Queen Charlotte's interest in portraiture in wax was proved by her appointment in 1801 of Catherine Andras to be her Modeller in Wax, Catherine being resident in London.

The exhibition's second documented visit to London was in 1816, when its location was in the 'Royal Mercatorium'. This was an arcade or bazaar on the east side of fashionable St James's Street.

Two curious stories from local history date from these early years of touring, when Marie must have required some breaks from travel to repair and refurbish current figures and create new portraits. There is a tradition in the history of Chalfont St Giles in Buckinghamshire that Madame Tussaud lived for a time at a house called Cottrell's Close and made some of her portrait figures there. Norwood, the London suburb, also has an intriguing claim that she had a residence there for some time during her early years in England. Here she is linked with an enigmatic woman called Mrs Mary Nesbitt, who was reputedly mysteriously involved in the Royalist cause during the French Revolution. There was a naval officer, Augustus John Hervey, who succeeded his uncle as Earl of Bristol in 1775. He was separated from his wife and set up house with Mrs Mary Nesbitt, an attractive young widow. When the Earl died in 1779 he left considerable property to Mrs Nesbitt including the large and beautiful house and park in Norwood in which they had lived.

Mary Nesbitt, very comfortably off, had many friends in high places, and became increasingly considered an influence behind the political scene. The *Morning Chronicle* of 2 September 1797 has an article about Mary Nesbitt which states 'her involvement with matters of British diplomacy concerning the French Royalists in 1793 and after the Directory in 1795 is obvious'. She is said to have acted as an agent for Prime Minister Pitt, and to have visited Paris several times, dressed as a man, and equipped with British gold for her missions in connection with the Royalist cause. Legend has it that Mary Nesbitt had contact in Paris with Marie Grosholtz (as Madame Tussaud was at the time, for she did not marry till the autumn of 1795), and aided her when she brought the exhibition to London in 1802. Mary Nesbitt is said to have found her a house, Effingham Lodge, not far from her own residence on Central Hill. It is from this base that Marie set off on her extensive travels with the exhibition. Certainly Mrs Nesbitt, with her connections in high places, would have been a most useful friend while Marie was seeking to establish her reputation and prestige at the Lyceum Theatre.

In 1810 Marie was back in Edinburgh, the scene of her first independent success, albeit still hampered then by her contract with Philipstal and his distasteful presence with his own show. Now she was completely free. The exhibition was located at the Panorama in Leith Walk, opposite the Botanic Gardens. The detailed and enthusiastic poster that she issued for this visit is the earliest to survive. The portrait figures listed show a combination of old and new. Very new was the portrait of Napoleon's Empress, Princess Marie Louise of Austria, whom he had married in April 1810. Her predecessor, the charming Josephine, discarded for her failure to produce an heir, had happily given Marie sittings for a portrait from life. Josephine's portrait figure had been brought over from Paris, but was now out of the picture. A new likeness of Prince Charles Stuart, Bonnie Prince Charlie, was surely modelled to please the Scottish visitors. There was also Marie's first recorded portrait of Mary, Queen of Scots. Their Majesties King George III and Queen Charlotte of England were grouped nearby, while Lord Nelson and Sir John Moore, the commander who had been mortally wounded defeating Napoleon's army at Corunna in Spain in 1809, were joined by prominent English and

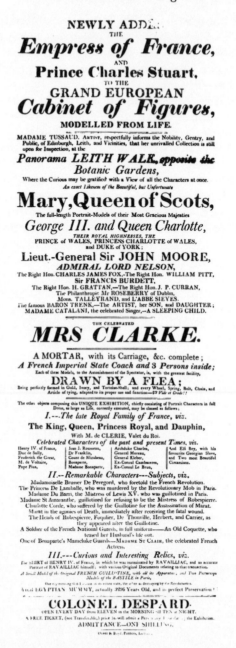

Poster of 1810/11 when Madame Tussaud's exhibition paid another visit to Edinburgh. *Madame Tussaud's Archives.*

Irish politicians. Napoleon himself, modelled from life by Marie at Josephine's request when he was First Consul, stood with some of his generals around him.

Marie did not neglect lesser personalities who were enjoying some contemporary fame, such as a Mr Roseberry of Dublin, noted for his philanthropy. The French Revolution however remained the heart of the exhibition, with the Royal Family of France and the guillotined heads of Revolutionaries Robespierre, Hébert, Carrier and Fouquier-Tinville.

Among the 'curios' the Egyptian mummy had survived its travels, and Marie felt the tiny ivory and tortoiseshell carriages drawn by fleas still had novelty appeal. The likeness of Colonel Edward Marcus Despard still held the public interest, though this conspirator's execution had taken place six years earlier. Marie had modelled his face after death during her stay at the Lyceum Theatre. Scandal was represented too. The name of Mrs Mary Ann Clarke appeared on the poster in large print. This notorious lady was the mistress of the Duke of York when Marie first modelled her portrait in 1803. She lived in great style in Cumberland Place. Now she was prominently in the news for in 1809 the Duke of York was charged in the House of Commons with wrong use, due to his mistress's influence and prompting, of his power of military patronage. Mrs Clarke's beauty, and the fortitude, even sauciness, with which she stood up to long examination at the Bar of the House had, in fact, won her many admirers. Her celebrity caught the public attention even in Scottish Edinburgh. Marie's journalistic flair, learnt from her 'uncle' Curtius, had developed since she landed in England and began her travels. It remained with her to the end of her life. The late writer H. V. Morton said in 1938, in an article for the *Daily Herald*, that Madame Tussaud was 'animated to the end by an extraordinary journalistic genius,' and nowhere does this gift demonstrate itself better than during the long years of touring with the exhibition. Any social historian seeking to know who people were talking about at this time can find valuable guidance in the exhibitions' surviving catalogues, posters and handbills.

It was this factor that made a visit by Madame Tussaud's exhibition an occasion of special importance. In the first three decades of the nineteenth century many people in small towns, with no local press, never saw a newspaper. The mail services were inefficient and expensive. It was not till 1840 that the 'penny post', the result of Sir Rowland Hill's reforms, brought better service. News had to travel to many areas by word of mouth from travellers and correspondence. Famous names were heard, important events and rumours discussed. When Madame

Tussaud's exhibition arrived people came from all around to see what some of these famous names looked like, and to learn something of the events in which they were involved, whether historical or contemporary. Few local newspapers carried illustrations, but here were these figures, correctly dressed and posed in 'the closest approximation of life'.

One of the earliest catalogues to survive was printed in Cambridge in 1819. Like its successors it is a compendium of information about the personalities portrayed in the exhibition and the happenings with which they were concerned. Marie set out her objectives in a short introduction:

> Madame Tussaud, in offering this little Work to the Public, has endeavoured to blend utility and amusement. The following pages contain a general outline of the history of each character represented in the Exhibition which will not only greatly increase the pleasure to be derived from a mere view of the Figures, but will also convey to the minds of young persons much biographical knowledge – a branch of education universally allowed to be of the highest importance.

Such a catalogue, carried to some isolated hamlet, would be read aloud to those who could not decipher it themselves. Topical and historical information was thus widely disseminated for it was not only townsfolk who visited the exhibition. People came in from miles around, and from time to time Marie's advertisements announce that owing to inclement weather she will remain a few days longer for the benefit of those who for this reason have been prevented from visiting. While this also made good commercial sense Marie's desire that as many as possible should *benefit* from seeing her wax portraits is always consistent.

Often special prices were offered to the poorer sections of the community so that they should not miss this opportunity. At the same time, always something of a snob with her 'ancien régime' image, Marie made sure that mingling the 'classes' should cause no embarrassment. In an advertisement of 1830, when the exhibition was set up in an elegant Assembly Rooms, the management announced:

> . . . considering that a large class of persons are unavoidably excluded from viewing the Collection owing to the pressure of the time they have arranged to admit

THE WORKING CLASS
During the time the Exhibition remains
FOR HALF PRICE
FROM A QUARTER BEFORE NINE TILL TEN IN THE EVENING

By this arrangement sufficient time will be given for the Classes to view the collection without interfering with each other and they hope that none but those so situated will take advantage of it as, if known, they will be refused.'

Even half-price at 6d must have been a strain on a working-class budget of the time and many workers would have retired exhausted long before a quarter to nine in the evening. Nonetheless the social and educational value of the exhibition should not be underestimated. Marie had lived and worked in the *Salon de Cire* in Paris throughout the French Revolution when ordinary working folk thronged in to see such portraits as that of Marat lying stabbed in his bath.

LAST WEEK BUT ONE

Exhibition and Promenade,

NOW OPEN WITH GENERAL APPROBATION,

In the Assembly Room, Green Row, Portsmouth.

MADAME TUSSAUD and SONS return their thanks for the support their Exhibition has met with, and they respectfully announce, that it must FINALLY CLOSE IN A FEW DAYS; at the same time considering that a large class of persons are unavoidably excluded from viewing the Collection, in consequence of the pressure of the times, they have made arrangements to admit

THE WORKING CLASS

During the time the Exhibition remains

For Half Price,

From a QUARTER BEFORE NINE TILL TEN in the Evening; by this arrangement, sufficient time will be given for both classes to view the Collection without interfering with each other, and they hope that none but those so situated, will take advantage of it, as, if known, they will be refused.

*** *Admittance* 1s.; *Children under Eight 6d.; Half price for the Working Class at a Quarter before Nine; no Half-price for Children.*

MADAME TUSSAUD AND SONS

Portsmouth 1830. Madame Tussaud made a practice of letting in people of 'The Working Class' for half price at certain hours in line with her educational policy. *Portsmouth Central Library.*

Throughout her travels Marie did not neglect donations to charity either. Often they benefited local charities, such as a special 'benefit' opening of the exhibition in aid of the Leeds Infirmary, which was reported in the *Leeds Mercury* of 27 May 1820. Sometimes these charitable contributions reflected the hardships of the time. One such was donated in 1822 at Shrewsbury when the proceeds of the opening day of the exhibition were given for the benefit of 'the

distressed peasantry of Ireland' where potato famines caused continuing misery. Another charity which gained support was the Fund for
Distressed Manufacturers, in York. Marie was showing in the Assembly
Rooms in 1824. On 23 December a pre-Christmas ball was taking
place in the room adjoining that in which the exhibition was set out.
While the dancers retired from the ballrooms to take tea Joseph cut
away the canvas screen separating the two rooms and allowed the ball
guests into the exhibition. The takings that evening amounted to
£15 10s, and this sum was donated without any deduction to the
Distressed Manufacturers. The receipts of the first evening in the
Exchange Rooms at Manchester, on 4 December 1821, were given to
aid the House of Recovery. Announcing this donation the local paper,
the *Exchange Herald*, added some information about the patients in
this charity hospital: 'House of Recovery. Admitted 4 – discharged
cured 5 – dead 1 – remain in House 10.'

Joseph's piano lessons had borne fruit and he proved musical.
Marie promoted the use of music during her years of travelling. She is
sometimes said to be the originator of the Promenade Concert.
Visitors made a 'splendid promenade' through the groups of figures
during evening openings to the accompaniment of music, a feature
that was stressed in the announcements. The first experiment may
well have been music played on the piano by Joseph himself while
visitors circulated. The first mention of a hired band came in November 1819 when Marie was at the Old Assembly Rooms, Derby. Her
advertisement of 10 November announced that a band would be in
attendance, and on the 24th the *Derby Mercury* reported:

> Madame Tussaud's exhibition of COMPOSITION FIGURES con-
> tinues to attract numerous parties to the Old Assembly Rooms,
> particularly in the evening when the room is brilliantly illuminated.
> The striking effect of the Figures is much enhanced and the atten-
> dance of a band of music renders it a very gay and interesting
> promenade.

Whenever circumstances made it possible this evening promenade
to a military or a quadrille band was henceforward an established
feature, and sometimes singers were added. At York, in 1826, there
were two of these, a Miss Bradbury and a Mr Bellamy while the leader
of the band was Mr Fisher, late of Norwich. Perhaps Mr Fisher had
joined Marie's entourage the previous year when she visited Norwich,
and remained with her for a while to organise the music. Under Mr
Fisher's baton the band seemed to take on added importance at York.
When the exhibition opened there at the beginning of November the

Promenade Concert, with vocal offerings included, began at 7 p.m. when a military band struck up. During Marie's two month stay in York visitors had the opportunity to listen to no less than five Benefit Concerts in the exhibition. The first two of these were for the two vocalists. Mr Fisher's Benefit Concert was enjoyed by no less than 600 people.

The success of these evenings encouraged Joseph to mount one for himself. This was advertised giving the full programme of music and, never one to miss an opportunity, Marie announced on 3 December that her own Benefit Concert would take place the following Tuesday. Occasionally Marie allowed her musicians to give an outside perfor- mance. One such occasion occurred the following year at Durham, in May when one of Mozart's Grand Masses was performed by Madame Tussaud's Band at the opening of the new Catholic Chapel. Though not a demonstratively religious woman, Marie never lapsed from the faith into which she had been born and baptized in Strasbourg in 1761.

This tradition of music in the exhibition, firmly established by Marie during her years of travel, was continued when she finally settled in London. It continued through the decades until the disastrous fire of 1925 which gutted the famous building. The new structure that arose from the ashes included a cinema where Würlitzer organ concerts carried on the musical tradition till that, in turn, was destroyed by a bomb during the Blitz of 1940. The organ in the cinema, however, could not produce the atmosphere created when the original bands and singers performed while visitors promenaded among the brightly illuminated wax figures in elegant Assembly Rooms around the country.

Marie's surviving advertisements, posters, handbills, editorial men- tions and catalogues of the period reflect her tireless striving for topicality, and for the improvement and establishment of her exhibi- tion. A constant updating of portraits of royalty, famous politicians, and public figures of many nationalities enlivened the exhibition, but Marie did not neglect persons of lesser and more transient fame. One of these was the master-manufacturer of patent medicines, Dr Solomon of Liverpool, a minor celebrity.

Dr Solomon's *Balm of Gilead* was a highly favoured remedy for a range of ills. In those days of the East India Company it was said that no ship sailed from Liverpool to India without consignments of this remedy for the exiled English and people of other nationalities who endured the hazards of climate and disease. When Marie paid her first visit to Liverpool in 1813 she sought and was granted a sitting by Dr Solomon. He lived in a splendid mansion built with the proceeds of his remedies some ten years earlier. Local history relates that, following the procedures she had practised so often, she spread the plaster for the life mask over the Doctor's carefully oiled face. In a most uncharacteristic fluster she was slow to insert the quills in his nostrils through which he would breathe while the plaster set. Dr Solomon bore his discomfort for a minute or two then tore the plaster from his face crying, 'By God, Madam, do you wish to smother me?' No amount of persuasion, it was said, would persuade Dr Solomon to have the process repeated, but either Marie did succeed in calming him, or she modelled him from observation and measurement, for Dr Solomon's portrait figure was added to the exhibition, and was still there when Marie exhibited in the Magnificent Mercatorium in St James's, London three years later.

The opportunity to model a famous personage visiting from abroad was seldom missed. In June 1814 the Emperor of Russia, Alexander I, visited London after the triumphant entry and stay in Paris of the Allied Commanders following Napoleon's defeat with his terrible retreat from Moscow in 1812 and subsequent capture and exile on the island of Elba. Vociferous crowds at Dover cheered the Emperor on his arrival. When Alexander I of Russia reached London he refused to take up the lodging prepared for him in splendid St James's Palace. Instead he joined his sister, the Grand Duchess Catherine, whose eccentric behaviour was shocking English society. She was living at the Pultney Hotel. Marie modelled the Emperor's portrait *Taken from life when in England* in the same year. If she had travelled to London from the West Country, leaving the exhibition there in charge of Joseph, now sixteen, Alexander might indeed have granted a brief sitting. Peter the Great had been modelled in wax, and Curtius had made a portrait of the Tsarevitch Paul of Russia who had visited the *Salon de Cire* in Paris when on his travels abroad. Alexander was renowned for his affability and informality, as well as being somewhat eccentric like his sister. In any case Marie had plenty of opportunity to observe the Emperor, for he readily showed himself to the public. Great crowds gathered round the Pultney Hotel to watch his comings and goings. Jane Austen the famous contemporary novelist wrote to her sister Cassandra who was staying in London, 'Do not be trampled to death running after the Emperor.' After he had returned to St Petersburg on 24 July, visitors to Madame Tussaud's exhibition could gaze as long as they liked at his waxen effigy, flanked by one of his Cossacks, named as Alexander Zemlenutin, in the picturesque Cossack uniform.

A year later, after the Battle of Waterloo in 1815, Marie modelled her second portrait of Napoleon Bonaparte, 'taken while he was on

In 1814 Madame Tussaud was showing in Bristol. The poster emphasized the Royal patronage she valued. *Madame Tussaud's Archives.*

board the *Bellerophon* in Torbay', Napoleon being on his way to his final exile in St Helena. Marie could possibly have used that earlier session, when Josephine had wished for her husband's portrait while he was First Consul, to gain access to the decks of the *Bellerophon*. The vessel was surrounded by scores of small craft loaded with sightseers, crowding in as close as they could to catch a glimpse of the finally defeated 'Boney' in the flesh, to stare at the ogre who had for so long threatened the shores of England.

Marie kept the spectrum of the exhibition wide, and sometimes a fortuitous opportunity led to the introduction of a new and un-expected addition. One such was the portrait of the Swedish theologian and philosopher Emanuel Swedenborg. He had died in London in 1772, regarded by several thousand followers as a spiritual seer. When in Manchester Marie had come across a gentleman who possessed an excellent portrait of Swedenborg, who still had a considerable following, painted when he was aged eighty-one, three years before his death. From this she modelled her own likeness of the man whose writings some regarded still as a revelation. Marie must have been particularly satisfied with her work as, although Sweden-borg's popular appeal was obviously limited, his figure remained in the exhibition for twenty-five years.

1820 was a year in which Marie twice acted with characteristic swiftness to ensure that a portrait was added to the display while the original was what today would be called 'hot news'. In Leeds the exhibition remained open a few days longer than originally announced so that its citizens could gaze at the likeness of Arthur Thistlewood who devised what was known as the Cato Street conspiracy. With nine colleagues he planned to assassinate the entire Cabinet. On his accession on 29 January 1820 the new King George IV had applied to his Ministers for a divorce from his Queen Caroline, from whom he had been separated for years and who was living abroad. In June she returned to England to the acclaim of the middle and lower classes who mostly regarded her as a sorely injured woman. Feeling ran high when it became known that the Cabinet were preparing what amounted to a Bill of Divorce. Thistlewood and his companions, one of whom proved to be an *agent provocateur*, plotted at a house in Cato Street to blow up the entire Cabinet while its members sat at dinner. This plan was revealed and most of the conspirators arrested at Cato Street where they were about to attempt to carry out their intention. Five, including Arthur Thistlewood, were hanged, others transported. Though the plot had little political significance it caused a great stir throughout the country. So strong were the feelings both in Parliament, and in the country, that the proposed Bill was hurriedly dropped by the Prime Minister, Lord Liverpool. Instead the Queen was voted an annuity of £50,000 a year. She did not live long to enjoy it as she died in July 1821.

Arriving in Manchester in August 1820 Marie opened the exhibition in the Large Room at the Exchange, with ninety figures. Here she introduced her portrait of 'S. Bergami' (sic) an Italian alleged to have been Queen Caroline's lover. Residing in exile on Lake Como Caroline had appointed Signor Bartolomeo Bergamo first as her courier, then as her equerry, and finally as her Chamberlain. Imprudently she allowed him to become her constant companion even at the dinner table. It was said that she showered favours on him, even procuring him several honours. Investigations were made by a special commission. As a result a Bill to deprive Caroline of her rights as Queen Consort and to dissolve her marriage to King George IV was introduced in the House of Lords. The examination of witnesses began on 21 August 1820. The Queen was ably and eloquently defended by Henry Brougham, already renowned for his ability as a lawyer. The accusations against her were refuted, and Henry Brougham gained immense popularity with the people if not with the King. Marie did not, however, model his portrait until ten years later when he was raised to the peerage.

As for Queen Caroline Marie had first modelled her in 1808, the same year she modelled King George III and Queen Charlotte. Caroline was then Princess of Wales though separated from her husband and living by herself at Shooters Hill and Blackheath, the object of much popular sympathy. Her conduct there had been imprudent, leading to a 'Delicate Investigation' into her behaviour, but she was found to have done nothing wrong. Marie referred to this situation discreetly in the catalogue: 'The separation of the Royal Pair – an event greatly to be deplored – is too delicate a subject to be entered into.'

As well as keeping abreast of events and personalities attracting public attention, and developing her skills in grouping and lighting so that the visitor, on entering, was at once struck by the 'brilliant assemblage', Marie began to expand the exhibition. This was a foretaste of the elaborate tableaux, treasures and relics which made the exhibition such a splendid experience when she was finally settled in London.

The accession to the throne of George IV in January 1820 was the opportunity for her first spectacular presentation. In October of that year Marie announced in the *Manchester Exchange Herald* her presentation of a magnificent allegorical Coronation Group. A new portrait figure of George IV was modelled from a recent bust and 'universally allowed to be one of the best likenesses ever taken'. The setting reproduced the crimson-hung and gilded Throne Room at Carlton House. The construction of the elaborate throne 'got up' by Messrs Petrie and Walker had taken a considerable time. This new group, with the musical promenade in the evening made the exhibition a 'truly elegant' spectacle which aroused great interest and enthusiasm.

Encouraged by the response to this, the most elaborate group she had yet offered, Marie unveiled her first tableau in Liverpool in time for the Christmas season. It depicted the Coronation of Napoleon, after the famous painting by Jacques Louis David who in 1804 was appointed court painter to the Emperor Napoleon. There were seven figures in this tableau. Napoleon in his coronation robes was modelled in the act of placing the crown on his head, attended by a page. Josephine knelt at the foot of an altar, while the Pope, attended by Napoleon's uncle, Cardinal Fesch, gave a blessing. The group included two of Napoleon's Mamelukes (Egyptian attendants) in their colourful costumes.

At Birmingham, in 1822, a collection of pictures and sculpture was added to the exhibition. Marie's 'uncle' Curtius had always had pictures and other works of art in the *Salon de Cire* at No. 20 Boulevard du Temple.

The increasing complexity of portrait figures, settings and works of art must have created transport problems, but Marie now had the assistance of her second son, Francis, who she had left as two-year-old Françison when she set off for England 20 years earlier. According to family tradition he joined his mother when he was about twenty-one years old, and he would remain with the exhibition, in partnership with his elder brother Joseph, for the rest of his life.

Francis, brought up by his grandmother, Madame Grosholtz, had not succeeded in establishing himself in a career in Paris. He was first apprenticed to a grocer, and when this was not a success, to a maker of billiard tables where he learned to carve wood. This was a useful skill for the exhibition as the legs and arms of the figures, when not exposed to view, were carved from wood. Francis did not settle into constructing billiard tables either, and finally made his way to England to join his mother. There is no record as to how he succeeded in catching up with her, but he seems to have taken his place in running the exhibition without fuss or friction, though many years later he told his father in a letter that Joseph was always Marie's favourite as he had been with her when he was little. It is said that on arrival in England Francis was shocked and horrified to hear that his mother had just perished in a shipwreck. The rumour proved untrue and he made his way to Liverpool to join her.

This story is supported by evidence that Marie, who had survived danger at sea on her way to Edinburgh in 1803, and again moving the exhibition from Waterford to Dublin in 1804, did survive a dangerous shipwreck in 1822. On 23 June of that year she announced her last week of showing in Liverpool due to 'a particular engagement in Dublin'. The new King, George IV, was making a state visit to the Irish capital, and what better occasion could there be for Marie to make a return visit to the scene of her early successes with the fine Coronation Group a highlight of the exhibition? However she never did reach Dublin, and, after an interval, reopened in Liverpool. Her attempt was frustrated by perilous shipwreck.

The evidence lies in the records and recollections of the families of Fynes-Clinton and Mathew, published privately in 1928 under the title *Annals from our Ancestors*. These annals contain an astonishing account of Madame Tussaud's survival of a shipwreck. The author relates the story:

> Before finishing with the Ffaringtons (a collateral family), I had better relate the adventure of Madame Tussaud, which must have occurred before 1830. One stormy evening Mrs Ffarington (my great aunt) and her two daughters, Susan and Mary Hannah, with some guests staying in the house were sitting after their dinner in a room called the morning room, a comfortable apartment leading off the hall in the front of the house, Worden, Preston. They heard footsteps on the gravel outside and heard the bell ring and one of the servants go across the hall to the door. A colloquy seemed to be taking place amidst a babel of voices which no-one could understand. Mrs. Ffarington's curiosity was aroused and she went to the door herself where she found the butler was being addressed in voluble French by a party of people outside. She brought them inside and found them to be a little company of foreigners who had suffered shipwreck on their way to Dublin. The leader of the party was Madame Tussaud, a middle-aged lady who had fled from Paris during the Reign of Terror, after having been a favourite of the Royal Family and suspect in consequence, and having been forced by the Communists to exercise her art of wax modelling on the decapitated heads of many of their victims. She brought some of her models to London and started an exhibition there afterwards touring with them about the country.

> The shipwreck cast her and the survivors of her party on the

Lancashire coast and all her possessions went to the bottom except one small box which the unfortunate companions carried between them when they all started to walk to Preston which they were told was the nearest town. Darkness fell on them and they struggled along in the rain and wind soaked to the skin and caked with Lancashire mud. They mistook their road and instead of arriving at Preston they found themselves at the lodge gates of Worden. How they got past the lodge I don't know, but they arrived at the house as described and were taken in and housed. Supper was got ready and dry clothing and they turned out to be such charming and interesting people that their stay was prolonged for several days.

The small box contained miniature models of various historical figures, and Madame Tussaud announced her intention of setting to work at once on fresh life-size models of those that had been lost.

Mrs Ffarington took her upstairs to a room where a number of old chests were kept, full of old costumes which had belonged to former members of the family, and presented her with a good many of these to clothe her new figures and help her to re-start her exhibition. In addition to this Mrs John Mathew (Mrs Ffarington's step-sister) at North Shields also became interested in Madame Tussaud and gave her a quantity of valuable old Venetian point lace.

Although this story has some inaccuracies as to the circumstances in which Marie left Paris and came to London, it appears certain that Marie underwent some disaster off the coast of Lancashire. The miniatures in the salvaged box were no doubt the framed miniature wax portraits in relief, an art form in which Curtius was a skilled practitioner. They included those of Louis XVI, the Duc d'Orleans, and Voltaire on his deathbed, the latter portrait surviving to this day.

It is possible that Marie and her party met with this disaster sailing on the *Earl Moira* which, bound for Dublin, was shipwrecked on 8 August 1822 when not far out from Liverpool. Most of those on board were on the way to Dublin for His Majesty's visit and carried considerable property with them. The local papers the *Liverpool Mercury* and the *Preston Chronicle*, gave coverage to this event. In storm and heavy seas the *Earl Moira* struck first on Burbo Bank, and then, the Captain being drunk, on Wharf Bank, where it stuck, battered and washed by tremendous waves. The decks were torn apart and the mast fell. Many, including the Captain, were washed overboard and perished. A lifeboat and other craft put out to sea and rescued the remaining exhausted passengers, who were put ashore along the coast. None knew how many lives were lost as, according to contemporary accounts, neither the number of passengers nor their names had been recorded before the vessel left port. There were believed to have been about one hundred on board, of whom some fifty were rescued. Madame Tussaud may have been one of these, and the story of her shipwreck became family history in the Clinton-Fynes and Mathew records. As for Marie herself, she never set foot on deck again.

A second occasion when Marie nearly lost everything and was herself in danger came during the Bristol Riots which took place in October 1831. Madame Tussaud's exhibition had been in Bristol since August, a third visit to this town. She was successfully established in the Assembly Rooms, Prince's Street, and would have anticipated a normal and peaceful continuation of a few more weeks before proceeding to Bath. However political conditions caused rioting throughout the country. The House of Lords rejected the second Bill for the reform of Parliament, and Bristol was one of the many places where citizens decided to make their wishes clear through violent protest.

Although in Bristol the military were called in to control the protesting mobs, on Sunday 30 October the destructive, looting elements, reinforced by criminals who had been freed from the prisons, attacked Queen's Square. Felix Farley's Bristol Journal describes the situation in which Marie found herself, a situation that must have brought back to her mind the terrors of the French Revolutionary mobs:

> After the destruction of the North and conflagration of the West sections of the Square the inhabitants of Prince's Street were in a state of great alarm. Parties of ruffians proceeded to several of the houses to warn the inmates of their intention to burn their premises and some of them actually commenced operations. During this awful state of suspense among others Madame Tussaud and her family experienced the most painful anxiety. It was stated that among other places the Assembly Rooms were marked out for destruction containing at the time their valuable collection of figures. These, at an immense risk of injury, were partly removed as hastily as circumstances would permit. The house in which Madame T. lodged on the opposite side of the street was among the number that became ignited from the firing of the West side of the Square, and we regret to hear that the lady's constitution has received a very severe shock.

A negro servant assisted in keeping the rioters off while the figures were carried out, and a youth called William Muller was on the scene and made a water-colour sketch of it. This sketch was retained in the exhibition until, ironically, it was destroyed in the fire of 1925 when Madame Tussaud's exhibition in Marylebone was burned out. Fortunately a photograph of the picture had been taken, so the record of that dangerous day was not entirely lost.

Among the losses Marie would have sustained if the Bristol mob had succeeded in firing the Assembly Rooms were the contents of her 'Adjoining Room' or 'Separate Room', to be dubbed by *Punch* fifteen years later with its famous title 'The Chamber of Horrors'.

Guillotined heads and other gruesome items were shown in a separate room for which an extra charge was made. Ladies were advised to hesitate before entering. It was not until 1846 that 'Punch' dubbed it 'The Chamber of Horrors'. *Madame Tussaud's Archives.*

As well as the moulds for the guillotined heads of the King and Queen of France, and the Revolutionary leaders Robespierre, Carrier, Hébert, and Fouquier-Tinville, Marie had brought other historical but alarming figures and objects, when she crossed the Channel in 1802.

There was the horribly emaciated figure of the Comte de Lorge, which she had modelled on his release from twenty years imprisonment in the Bastille, and models of that prison-fortress and the guillotine. She also brought her portrait of Marat whom she had been called to model as he lay assassinated in his bath, and 'relics' such as the bloodstained shirt that Henry IV of France had been wearing when assassinated. This too had been in the *Salon de Cire* in Paris. The death head of Colonel Despard which Marie had taken during her stay at the Lyceum was still with the collection.

While Marie had never allowed the display of such less agreeable objects to spoil the 'coup d'oeil' and 'splendid assemblage' of figures that she arranged in so many venues during her years of travel, the question of space for their accommodation made adequate display a frequent problem. These figures and 'relics' needed a separate display as they had had in No. 20 Boulevard du Temple.

According to tradition it was a University don visiting the exhibition who uttered a strong condemnation, saying that it was both wrong and distasteful that Revolutionaries and other despicable characters should mingle, cheek by jowl, with portraits of fine and noble men and women. Marie took this criticism to heart. Whenever she could she managed to contrive a separate section for them. In 1822, when she was in Manchester, she announced that 'Highly interesting figures and objects in consequence of the peculiarity of their appearance are placed in an Adjoining Room and form a separate exhibition well worth the inspection of artists and amateurs.' The additional charge for admission to the Adjoining Room was 6d. In 1823, when Marie hired the Town Hall in Coventry and stayed for about three months, she used the Mayoress's Parlour as the Separate Room.

Additions were made from time to time as notorious crimes occurred. Among the biggest crowd-pullers were the portraits of Burke and Hare, the body-snatchers. They were brought to trial in Edinburgh at the end of December 1828. Burke was hanged on 28 January 1829 before an enormous crowd of spectators. Hare turned King's evidence and went free. Marie had opened the exhibition at the Pantheon, Church Street, Liverpool on the 16th of the month. It was her third visit and she planned a stay of several months. The trial and conviction of Burke provided her with an opportunity to catch the public interest.

On Friday 13 February she made her announcement:

NEW ADDITION
BURKE THE MURDERER

Madame Tussaud has the honour to announce that she has completed the figure of Burke which she hopes will meet with the approbation of her friends and the public although the introduction may be considered improper by *some* yet as it is done merely in compliance with the public curiosity she trusts it will be received with satisfaction. It represents him as he appeared at his trial and the greatest attention has been paid to give as good an idea as possible of his personal *appearance.*

Marie must have travelled to Edinburgh to sit in the court room, observing, noting and sketching, while her sons transported the exhibition from Preston, its previous venue. On the 19th of August, again in Edinburgh, a man known as Stewart and his wife were hanged for the murder of a sea-captain, whom they poisoned and robbed. They were alleged to have caused the death of nine other victims, first drugging them with laudanum and then robbing them. Mrs Stewart helped. She was the first woman criminal to appear in the exhibition since Marie brought it to England. There had been several in the 'Caverne des Grands Voleurs' in Curtius's *Salon de Cire* in Paris, and the Chamber of Horrors in London would provide place for a number more.

In spite of the shock she had sustained during the Bristol riots, Marie continued her relentless touring, though in 1831 she reached her seventieth birthday. Both her sons had by then married, Joseph to Elizabeth Babbington and Francis to Rebecca Smallpage. Nothing is known of where and how the sons met their future wives, but it was in the year that Marie reached seventy that her first grandchild was born, a boy named Joseph Randall. It was to this grandchild that control of the exhibition would eventually descend. He was the son of Francis and Rebecca.

In spite of increasing family responsibilities, the constant touring continued, both wives apparently taking a share in the work. There was no friction with their mother-in-law. In fact Marie seems to have maintained a remarkably harmonious group of workers during her years of travel. The late spring of 1833 found them first at Oxford, and then at Reading. In the latter town Marie seized the opportunity of modelling Dennis Collins, accused of attempted regicide, while he was in gaol there.

More pathetic than criminal, this former sailor, who had lost a leg during his service, had a pension grievance. Unable to get any help he hurled a stone at King William IV when the monarch was attending Ascot races in June 1832. The jagged flint that he threw hit the King's hat, but could have caused serious injury had it struck temple or eye. Collins was hustled off to Reading gaol amid uproar. Marie herself hastened there to take a mask of his face, and note his tattered sailor's garb. The wretched Collins protested that he had meant only to draw attention to his grievance, which involved a 10d a week pension, not to kill or injure. He was spared execution but sentenced to transportation for life.

King William IV had ascended the throne in 1830, and Marie set up an impressive Coronation group. This had six splendid figures as well as her portrait figure of the new King, and three allegorical figures representing England, Scotland, and Wales. The group was set beneath 'a magnificent canopy, surmounted by a large Fancy Coronet'. No more was heard of the miserable Dennis Collins who died during his voyage to exile, but his figure remained in the Chamber of Horrors for many decades.

The following year at Brighton Town Hall, Marie received a couple of Royal visitors, who she added to her list of patrons. They were Princess Augusta and Prince George of Cambridge, who she brought to see the famous exhibition. Afterwards the Princess graciously wrote: 'We have been offered much amusement and gratification.' Marie responded with an advertisement expressing publicly her thanks for this Royal favour. Marie had to stay longer in Brighton than she had planned, as the Magistrates of the town of Lewes refused permission for her to book the Town Hall in spite of her enhanced prestige, and there was no other suitable location available.

During the remainder of 1833 Marie made her way through Kent, showing at Canterbury, Dover, Maidstone and Rochester. Finally, in November, she arrived at the outskirts of London where a six week visit using large rooms at The Green Man, Blackheath, was planned. Though neither Marie nor her two sons, now stalwart young men of thirty-three and thirty-one, both competent modellers in wax, were aware of it, the exhibition would never leave London again. The years of travelling were over and done with, though permanent settlement at premises known as Bazaar, Baker Street, was still over a year away.

Marie remained at the Assembly Rooms in The Green Man until 17 December. It was a successful visit. Blackheath had become quite fashionable since the late Caroline, then Princess of Wales, had lived there for some time before going into exile on the Continent. The Green Man was a long-established and picturesque inn, patronized by upper-class excursionists and holiday-makers from central London and provided Assembly Rooms for use by local residents. However, the winter months were not conducive to excursions, and Marie did not linger there. She decided to move on to a more populous location, and in an advertisement announced that, though grateful for the kind support received in Blackheath, the exhibition must close and move to the Old London Bazaar, Gray's Inn Road, King's Cross. Marie respectfully solicited the recommendation of those who had friends in the metropolis.

After the Christmas break the exhibition opened in this new location, the buildings of which surrounded three sides of a square. In 1826 it had been the London Horse and Carriage Repository, and three years later was established as a Bazaar, a collection of small selling enterprises. These had included in 1832 social reformer Robert Owen's short-lived National Equitable Labour Exchange, a system by which goods were bartered without the use of cash. On the first floor there were a number of large rooms with tall windows, including an Assembly Room which, said Marie in an advertisement, was the only one to accommodate her assemblage of figures.

In these central premises the exhibition made a highly satisfactory impact. One press report described it as 'one of the most remarkable exhibitions that has been seen in London for a considerable period'. The writer of the long description that followed was evidently not an admirer of most wax portraiture, for he specially praised Madame Tussaud and her sons for their bold efforts to overcome 'the vapid velvet faces and unspeculating eyes' usually characteristic of portraits modelled in this medium. He also remarked on the evident care and expense with which the large rooms had been prepared. One end was occupied by William IV's Coronation group, and the tableau of Napoleon's Coronation was at the other, with many figures arranged between. In the midst of these was a figure of Madame Tussaud herself wearing one of her bonnets and a silk cloak. Visitors were uncertain, so life-like was it, whether this was the proprietress in the flesh or not.

As usual particular attention had been paid to the lighting and the reporter was impressed: 'When the whole is aided by the effect of lamplight it becomes highly interesting: the mellow artificial illumination throwing a deeper tone over the flesh colour in the figures, and rendering the glare of the glass eyes less remarkable.' There was a Second Room, 'that ghastly apartment', with the death heads, murderers, and relics. Into this ladies were advised not to enter. But they could enjoy a musical accompaniment to the morning and afternoon promenades provided by the Messrs Tussaud and the Fishers.

It was really the first time Marie had been able properly to display her artistry since she left Paris, and she remained at Gray's Inn Road for five successful and profitable months. During this period a purchase was made which was the harbinger of the Napoleon Rooms that were later to become famous. On 22 March Napoleon's eagles, which were carried into battle with the flag were acquired for £12 13s 7d at a sale of Waterloo spoils.

The exhibition would move back to Gray's Inn Road at the end of 1834, but in the meantime the next venue was the Lowther Rooms. These formed part of the Lowther Arcade in King William Street at the West end of the Strand, an area already familiar to Marie from her beginning at the Lyceum Theatre, back in 1802, when she had embarked on her English enterprise.

The Arcade, also known as the Lowther Bazaar, was operated by Messrs Graves and Young. For some years it had featured various kinds of entertainment as well as its principal activity, the sale of fancy goods. Marie used the *Morning Post* to advertise her exhibition in the Lowther Rooms. She reminded patrons that the exhibition was 'admirably calculated to induce youth to make themselves acquainted with History and Biography'. It was open from eleven in the morning till six in the evening, and again from seven till ten. The band played during the evening promenade.

In August another move was made to Grove House, Camberwell. This was situated in one of the numerous pleasure gardens, large and small, which still flourished in London during the first three or four decades of the nineteenth century. The Old Grove House functioned as both an inn and a hotel, and had an adjoining coachyard, so was a well-frequented place. The building included a spacious room with three tall windows. In this agreeable spot, popular with Londoners, Marie spent the summer and early autumn moving towards the end of October to the Mermaid Tavern, Hackney, a distance of only about seven miles.

The Mermaid stood on the West side of the High Street, easily accessible, and the Assembly Rooms were connected to the tavern by a covered way. They were patronized by the many gentry living in the neighbourhood. The tavern itself had large grounds which included two bowling greens, one of which was also used for archery. A shaded 'dark walk' skirted the kitchen garden and a brook ran through the grounds. Though these rural attractions were less appealing at the time of year when Marie arrived, they lent the place prestige.

The visit proved successful and the two week's planned stay was extended. The exhibition was 'brilliantly illuminated' from eight in the evening, and the music began at half past seven. There was daytime opening as well, and Marie was able to advertise that the exhibition had been received 'with the most brilliant reception since its arrival in Hackney, the Assembly Rooms being completely filled every evening with the most respectable company'. She stayed on at Hackney until Christmas.

During these weeks a return to Gray's Inn Road was being actively planned. The large room there, 70 ft by 46 ft was to present a new and exciting spectacle, with 'a Magnificent and Unequalled Portable Decoration, superior to any ever exhibited, representing a Golden Corinthian Saloon'. This striking project had been designed by Marie's younger son Francis, who had now been with his mother for fourteen years. Credit was given in the advertisements to the craftsmen who had carried out the work. Mr Bielefeld was responsible for the elaborate papier mâché decoration, while the joinery was carried out by Mr Hunt of 22 Berwick Street. The glory of this new setting was the gilding, in burnished and matt finish, created with maximum effect by Mr Syffert of 55 Great Queen Street. In all there were 2,000 feet of gilding and the whole structure 'any description of which must fall short of reality' had cost more than £1,100, a very considerable sum.

In this superb setting were placed the Coronation group and the Napoleonic tableau, with a large array of figures which included that of the popular Duke of Sussex and another of the novelist, Sir Walter Scott, modelled by Marie in Edinburgh in 1828. While there she had attended the trial of Burke and Hare, the body snatchers, which began on 24 December of that year. In spite of the elaborate and expensive new setting, the price of admittance remained at 1/- with children under eight half price. The Second Room, with 'highly interesting figures and objects' cost an extra 6d, as did the Biographical Catalogue.

29 December was the opening date for the most important presentation ever attempted hitherto by Marie and her sons. The 'coup d'oeil' when the room was lit up was reported as particularly striking, while 'pleasing modern music' was played morning and evening.

The large room at Bazaar, Gray's Inn Road, had been booked for three months. Then a move had to be made. The 'Portable Decoration' had to be transported to a new location, a building also known as Bazaar but situated at the junction of Baker Street and Portman Square. This building, though neither Marie nor her sons realised it at the time, would be the home of the exhibition not only for the rest of Marie's lifetime, but until the year 1884.

CHAPTER V

The London Establishment

THE premises to which Madame Tussaud's exhibition now moved had formerly been the King Street Barracks. They had then comprised the barracks and stabling of the Royal Life Guards. According to local report a regiment of the Life Guards had marched out of the King Street entrance en route to fight in the battle of Waterloo in 1815. Later the barracks were abandoned and the buildings put to other uses. They became known as Bazaar, Baker Street, Portman Square. Marie, with her sons Joseph and Francis, took over a large room on the first floor which was believed to have served originally as the Mess Room of the Life Guards. Some useful buildings jutted out from it, and with a private house facing across Baker Street it provided convenient accommodation for both exhibition and family.

An area at the back of Bazaar had previously been used for the sale of horses, but now in 1835 carriages and a variety of household goods were on sale there. The products of the Panklibanon Iron Works, whose sale room adjoined the exhibition's spacious room, were typical of the type of merchandise sold in the vicinity, which attracted a steady flow of customers to Baker Street. The Panklibanon advertised extensively and the goods they sold included 'general furnishing ironmongery, best Sheffield plate, German silverware'; papier mâché tea trays, tea and coffee urns, stoves, grates, kitchen ranges, fenders, fire-irons and baths of all kinds – shower, cold, vapour and plunge – were sold alongside garden engines, which were always kept on hand by the proprietors of the establishment, and patent 'radiant stoves'. Busy showrooms like these, with well-off customers, were useful neighbours.

Entertainment was not new in Bazaar. As early as 1829 there had been 'magnificent Exhibitions of Musical and Mechanical Automata', which had proved very popular. The large room that Marie had secured was well adapted to entertainment purposes. Other diversions in the neighbourhood also attracted people to the area. Not far away in Regents Park a Diorama had been established for more than a decade. This was a spectacular painting, often circular, which by use of lights directed on or through it produced the effect of natural phenomena such as sunrise or moonlight. It had been owned in 1823 by Louis Daguerre, himself originally a painter in Paris, who was to become famous for his pioneering work in photography. Although the Diorama was now in other hands, and its popularity beginning to wane, it still brought many people to the locality.

Bazaar was conveniently placed for transport. Horsebus proprietors were working the Oxford Street routes nearby. In 1836 they were banded into the London Conveyance Co. whose routes included New Road, now a part of Marylebone Road. The horse-buses offered opportunities for advertising and Marie was one of the first to make use of them. She had always believed in the value of suitable publicity and in 1836 had no fewer than 400 posters and 500 handbills printed.

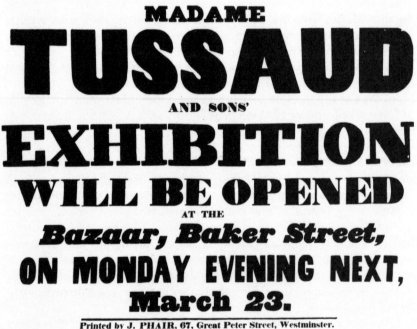

MADAME
TUSSAUD
AND SONS'
EXHIBITION
WILL BE OPENED
AT THE
Bazaar, Baker Street,
ON MONDAY EVENING NEXT,
March 23.

Printed by J. PHAIR, 67, Great Peter Street, Westminster.

In 1835 Madame Tussaud and her sons ceased travelling and opened the permanent London exhibition in premises known as Bazaar, Baker Street, Portman Square. *Madame Tussaud's Archives.*

When the move took place, on 15 March 1835, an extra 'caravan' and horses had to be hired to transport the Golden Corinthian Saloon, the portrait figures, and all the related material from Gray's Inn Road to Baker Street. Though the exhibition opened up in a comparatively short time, it was not until June that the extensive re-planning was completed. On 1 June *The Times* wrote a very satisfactory report:

> Madame Tussaud's Exhibition: A completely new arrangement of the figures which comprise this splendid exhibition has taken place, and the effect is much improved. . . . The effigies of many of the great have not, like the originals, absolutely turned their coats, but they have been accommodated with suits that are more in keeping with their characters than when they were first exhibited to the public . . . the whole appearance on entering, especially in the evening when the whole is brilliantly illuminated, is peculiarly imposing and splendid.

The *Court Journal* also made special comment on the lighting: 'When the spacious room is brilliantly lighted up, and the strains of music enchant the ear, this is a scene for a pleasant and instructive hour.' The promenade lasted from seven-thirty till ten in the evening and the music was provided by Messrs Tussaud and Fisher. At last Marie had achieved a Salon that could rival the former *Salon de Cire* which had been her 'uncle' Curtius's pride.

This impressive setting and 'unequalled coup d'oeil' soon led to illustrious patrons. In July the *Morning Herald* announced that His Royal Highness the Duke of Sussex had honoured Madame Tussaud with a visit to Bazaar, Baker Street. The Duke of Wellington was an important visitor. No doubt he was particularly interested in the new Napoleonic Group, entitled 'Great Men of the late War' which included his own portrait for which he had given sittings. The Duke became a regular visitor and asked to be informed when a portrait figure of particular interest was added. The Duke of Sussex also permitted a new likeness to be taken.

The entrance fee to the expanded exhibition remained unchanged, 1/- for adults, 6d for children and an extra 6d for the Separate Room, so grisly that only the boldest ladies ventured in. It was soon to have a new denizen, the would-be Corsican assassin Joseph Fieschi. He was a minor French government official, dismissed for fraud, who hatched a plot to assassinate Louis Philippe, King of the French, as he rode through the streets of Paris with his son and royal party. Fieschi constructed for the purpose an 'infernal machine', a contraption with 25 gun barrels that could be fired. On 28 July 1835 he managed to discharge this from a hiding-place as the King passed by. He only wounded the King's horses, but eighteen people were killed. Fieschi was seized and guillotined the following February. In addition to the portrait figure of the assassin, Joseph and Francis built a replica of the 'infernal machine', which caused a sensation in the Separate Room.

In spite of the general acclaim it seems Marie was still hesitant about staying too long in one location. For three decades she had always moved on, staying longer in large centres of population like Liverpool or Manchester, but never long enough for local interest to slacken. On a poster of 1836 she announced that the spacious room in which her figures were arranged to such advantage was only booked for a limited period. According to family tradition it was an event that occurred in the autumn of 1836, when she had been at Bazaar for nearly sixteen months, that convinced her that she no longer needed to take to the road again. It was the sudden, tragic death of the singer Maria Felicitas Malibran that caused Marie to change her policy.

Maria Malibran, daughter of the Spanish singer Manuel Garcia, was twenty-eight years old when she died suddenly, having already won herself considerable fame. Herself a singer, she possessed a rich melodious mezzo-soprano and remarkable power of dramatic characterization. Malibran had gone to New York with her father when she was seventeen and had married a French merchant, François Malibran there. His bankruptcy forced her to return to Europe and earn money through her singing. She made her début in London in 1825 and had a triumph in Paris in 1827 which brought her renown all over Europe. In 1836 she was appearing at a festival in Manchester, when she was taken ill and died on 23 September. The unexpected and early death of this young singer shocked the public, for she had made an exceptional impact during her short career. Marie immediately set to work to model her portrait. There were many pictures of her.

As soon as the figure was placed in the exhibition people flocked in to see the singer in wax, 'the nearest approximation to life'.

Marie had 500 posters printed advertising Madame Malibran's portrait. A surviving ledger shows that the introduction of this figure and the publicity surrounding it, caused attendances to double during the ensuing weeks. Marie decided that with the growing population of London and modern transport which brought visitors to the capital from all parts of the country, it was no longer necessary to take her exhibition to the people. The people could now come to see her. A lease was negotiated and Bazaar became the home of Madame Tussaud's exhibition until 1884 when she herself had been dead for over thirty years.

It was thus, when she was seventy-five and her sons thirty-eight and thirty-six respectively that Marie found herself again living as she had lived at No. 20 Boulevard du Temple in Paris, with her exhibition at the heart of a great capital city. Her thoughts must have turned back to the policies her 'uncle' Curtius had pursued and in which he had trained her. She followed them still. The exhibition was always kept updated, it offered instruction as well as entertainment in an atmos-phere of brilliance in which past and present came together. Then, as had happened in Paris, the great and the humble, foreigners as well as native visitors, would be drawn to it.

When the formalities were finished and the premises at Bazaar could finally be regarded as a permanent setting, Marie could give the art of which she was so skilled an exponent its place in English culture. Not without reason would the Duke of Wellington call the exhibition 'the most entertaining place in London', nor *Chamber's Journal* remark, as it did in 1835, 'we can walk, as it were, along the plank of time'. In a settled abode a new era of development could begin no longer restricted by transport problems or the artistic curbs that a life of continuous travel imposed.'

Marie's successful new portrait of the Duke of Sussex was quickly followed by other royal likenesses. In 1836 she modelled 'from life' the young Princess Victoria and her mother the Duchess of Kent. There is a tradition that the Princess paid a visit to the exhibition before she became Queen, possibly to see the likeness of her uncle, the Duke of Sussex, as well as her own. Lord Melbourne, Prime Minister, and Joseph Hume, the radical reformer who, amongst other causes, advocated savings banks, and the abolition of flogging in the navy, were also modelled. Marie's impressive list of patrons now included Princess Augusta and Prince George of Cambridge, who had visited the exhibition in Brighton, Princess Sophia and the royal Dukes of Cumberland and Sussex. Also mentioned were Lords Brougham, Harroby, Auckland, and of course His Grace the Duke of Wellington. Marie was well prepared to set up a fine group on the accession of Princess Victoria to the throne on 27 June 1837.

This was followed in 1838 by a splendid Coronation Group. In the centre Queen Victoria was enthroned, wearing the crown and royal robes, holding orb and sceptre. The Archbishop of Canterbury 'im-plored a blessing' supported by the Archbishop of York and Lord

Bishop of London. The bevy of surrounding figures were all dressed 'in strict accordance with the regulations at the Coronation'. A drawing on the cover of a contemporary Catalogue illustrates the impressive sight that met Londoners and country and foreign visitors as they entered. Some foreign ambassadors were now added to the patronage list. The Coronation Group was placed in the centre of the long salon which had a coffered roof and elaborate plaster mouldings. Down each side of the hall gas chandeliers were suspended in long rows, illuminating the other groups and single figures arranged along the walls and in the middle. At the entrance end eight upholstered benches were arranged, so that visitors could sit down and marvel at the *coup d'oeil* before them. The artist and cartoonist George Cruikshank was one of those who sat down and gazed. He painted an aquatint with the caption 'View in Honour of the Coronation, Bazaar, Baker Street, Madame Tussaud's'. It was one of a series of ten large aquatints entitled *London Fashion Plates* depicting fashionable spots in London.

In Coronation year, 1838, *Madame Tussaud's Memoirs and Reminiscences of France* was published. Marie had not herself penned them. Among family friends was a family named Hervé who had settled in England at the end of the eighteenth century. Three of them were talented silhouettists, and one, François Hervé, an author and traveller. He had published an account of his experiences in Greece and Turkey. Marie was noted for her voluble conversation and fund of anecdotes and descriptions of personalities and events she had witnessed at Versailles and during the years of Revolution. With her trained, observant eye and ear, she was an accurate mental recorder of what she saw and heard and her powers were not diminished by her advancing years. While she never put pen to paper, François Hervé did, and meticulously noted down what she said. He then decided to put all this information and anecdote in its historical setting to produce what he called 'an abridged history of the French Revolution'. Hervé was not a trained historian and his dates sometimes went astray, but he produced a volume of vivid recollections covering her life in Paris and the *Salon de Cire* from the age of six until her departure from France in 1802.

One of François Hervé's brothers made a silhouette likeness of Marie, a tiny figure, no longer slender as she had been when a girl, her stoutness accentuated by her full bunchy skirt and large bonnet. But her alertness is unmistakable. Joseph no longer practised the art of silhouette-making in the exhibition (possibly he had originally learned it from the Hervés) but he used his skill again to make a

composite picture of a family group including his mother, in the same
pose as Hervé had taken her, and his wife seated at a harp.

The following year an innovation came to Bazaar, Baker Street, a
change that must have been regarded with very mixed feelings by
those who had established businesses there. The Royal Smithfield
Club decided to use the large open area at the back, where horses and
carriages had been sold in the past, as the venue for its first Cattle
Show. This influx of beasts had obvious disadvantages in the way of
dirt and smells, but on the other hand the show brought to London
hundreds of country visitors who otherwise might not have visited the
capital. Some, no doubt, would have seen Madame Tussaud's exhibition during its years of touring, for people coming in from the
countryside had always been an important proportion of the attendance during the years of touring.

Misgivings soon vanished, for the Cattle Show was outstandingly
successful. It remained a yearly feature of Bazaar until it moved to the
Agricultural Hall at Islington in 1861. Large poultry shows also took
place periodically, and as time went by amenities improved. Tarpaulin
roofing was replaced by a proper roof. By 1843, according to a
contemporary account, it could produce a rival *coup d'oeil* to Madame
Tussaud's exhibition. The spacious area now had a lofty, pointed roof
and much improved ventilation. The place was bright with flaring
gas-lights which illuminated 'vistas of beasts'. The layout was amended
and aisles widened so that ladies with their increasingly voluminous
skirts (which culminated in the crinoline) could move through the
show 'with perfect safety'.

The Prince Consort was an enthusiastic patron, and showed some
fine beasts. Queen Victoria visited the show in 1844, though she did
not climb the stairs to Madame Tussaud's exhibition. To Marie the
Cattle Show proved more of an advantage than a nuisance. She
welcomed the extra thronging visitors. 'Who does not remember dear
old Madame Tussaud,' wrote one who recalled those days, 'her sharp
twinkling eyes, eager look, and truly French style of doing the *aimable.*'

With the exhibition so busy Marie had neither time nor inclination
to take on extra work, no matter how flattering the request might be.
She was asked to undertake restoration work on the 'Ragged Regiment', the collection of wax effigies in Westminster Abbey that had
long been neglected. According to family history her reply was tart
and decisive. 'Voyez, Messieurs, I have a shop of my own to look after.'
In any case, since her split from her partner, Philipstal, so many years
ago, she had refused to work in the interests of any but herself and
her family.

There is some indication that in spite of her strong constitution and will-power Marie did now sometimes feel fatigued. In August 1839 her son Francis replied on her behalf to a letter from an admirer of the exhibition. This lady asked if Madame Tussaud would like a copy of a book on the 'Duc de Normandie', one of the pretenders who claimed that they were in fact the Dauphin, the child who, according to the Revolutionary authorities, had died while still imprisoned in the Temple in 1795. Francis wrote that his mother, owing to a long indisposition, found herself reduced to 'so nervous a state as to be unable to guide her pen'. Holding a pen was in fact an occupation in which Marie had never had the time nor the wish to indulge. Her sons could deal with irrelevant correspondence. However, Marie signed the letter herself, as the correspondent had particularly requested a reply in Madame Tussaud's own hand. Her signature, though perhaps less firm than when she had signed letters to her husband and family thirty years earlier, gave no indication of feebleness. Marie did not want the offered book. She said it had already been sent to her, 'and we have every reason to think from the Dauphin himself. She is of the opinion he is still in existence.' There were many Royalists who believed the little Dauphin had been smuggled out of the Temple prison, though no contender for the title of King Louis XVII of France ever substantiated his claim.

Queen Victoria's marriage to Prince Albert of Saxe-Coburg-Gotha took place in February 1840, and inspired a charming group. Albert was depicted in the act of placing the ring on his bride's finger. He wore a splendid field-marshal's uniform. Queen Victoria's dress was of real Honiton lace 'by Miss Sidney', whose name evidently meant something to the fashionable public. In the same year Charles Dickens published *The Old Curiosity Shop* with Mrs Jarley's Waxworks so clearly based on Madame Tussaud's travelling exhibition. There was an addition to The Separate Room when Edward Oxford, an insane youth, tried to assassinate the Queen and her husband as they drove along Constitution Hill. He fired two shots. Prince Albert pushed the Queen down, and the second went over her head. Oxford was found guilty but insane and sent to a secure lunatic asylum.

For Marie and her two sons, however, the most important event of the year was a purchase they decided to make. In October they acquired the Coronation robes of the late King George IV. The robes had been originally designed by the King himself, for his Coronation ceremony, and he was said to have paid £18,000 for them, a very large sum at the time.

George IV left very heavy debts when he died in 1830 and the robes

Handbill of 1846. The words relating to the display of Court dresses angered the editor of 'Punch' and inspired an article which gave 'The Chamber of Horrors' its name in perpetuity. *Madame Tussaud's Archives.*

were sold with the rest of his extensive wardrobe as a contribution towards paying them off. The new King, William IV, was not interested in them. He preferred something simpler for his own Coronation. The auction of 'His Majesty's Coronation Robes' was reported in *The Times* on 11 June 1831. The reporter stated at the end of his account of proceedings: 'There was very slight competition for any of the articles, and we did not observe that they were knocked down to a person of distinction.' Whoever did the bidding at the auction, it was not Marie herself, nor, it seems, her sons. At the time they were in the West Country with no apparent intention of settling permanently in London. Such cumbersome robes, though said to be in very good condition, would have been extremely difficult to handle while on the road. A ledger entry of 18 October 1840 records their purchase by Madame Tussaud's exhibition, but does not name the vendor.

It took six months to design and build an appropriate setting. In April 1841 the same ledger records 'Set up George IIII'. These four words describe the most ambitious project Marie and her sons had ever undertaken, 'acknowledged to be the most splendid sight ever seen by a British public'. Designed and supervised by Joseph and Francis, it was, they said, 'an attempt to do honour to his late Majesty's taste,' and certainly Marie, with her memories of the Court of Versailles must have felt more sympathy with George IV's flamboyant leanings than with the respectable bourgeois qualities that their Majesties, William IV and Queen Adelaide, had so obviously preferred.

Much public comment was naturally aroused, summed up by Mead in his book *London Interiors* where he illustrated the scene. A reporter was sent along by the widely circulated *Chambers Journal.* He was struck by the 'spacious recess or ante-room, the whole of which is seen at one glance [Marie's famous *coup d'oeil*] magnificently fitted up. The walls are hung in the richest manner with crimson silk velvet, and the floor laid with crimson, the whole got up in the most tasteful and superb style.' There were also 'unique' doors and joinery with elaborate papier mâché ornamentation created by a Mr Bielefeld, who did much work for Madame Tussaud, and quantities of gilding.

The likeness and attitude of the wax figure was based on Sir Thomas Lawrence's famous portrait of George IV in his Coronation robes. The robe he wore in the tableau was the one he had designed for the procession to Westminster Abbey. It was seven yards long and three yards wide, purple, richly embellished and ermine-lined. Arranged spectacularly on each side of the King's figure were the gold-embroidered Imperial Mantle, which the King had donned after his crowning for the journey back to Westminster Hall, and the Parliamentary robe that he subsequently wore for opening Parliament. It was claimed that these three robes contained in all 567 feet of velvet and embroidery and all three wraps had ermine lining.

Incorporated in the tableau was an ornate throne, a copy of the one used by George IV at Carlton House when, as Prince Regent, he received the allied sovereigns after the defeat of Napoleon. There were careful replicas of the Crown, Orb, and Sceptre. Mead called the tableau 'the focus of the gorgeous spectacle' offered by the whole exhibition.

The George IV tableau met with nothing but praise at the time, but in the future, after Marie's death it would arouse the ire of both Dickens and Thackeray. In 1854 Charles Dickens wrote an article entitled 'History in Wax' for his periodical *Household Words*. After describing George IV 'set up' in all his glory, he continued, 'It is in a tone of deep regret that our historian, speaking of these robes, observes "their like will never be seen again". I, for one, do most fervently hope and believe not.' Six years later Dickens still felt outrage when he looked at the robes: 'Here the writer would meekly ask whether there is not something compromising to the dignity of royalty in the sale of such wares, and their exhibition in this place.' Thackeray expressed an equal sense of outrage when he wrote in *The Four Georges* in 1861, 'Madame Tussaud has got King George's Coronation robes: is there any man alive now who would kiss the hem of such trumpery?' Soon after Thackeray's outburst the robes had to be removed from open display and put under glass as the heavily polluted atmosphere of Victorian London was causing deterioration.

Although George IV and his robes were arranged for maximum effect to draw in the crowds, Marie did not abandon the policy she had always followed of creating an atmosphere of participation and intimacy. A great attraction for visitors was the impression that they were mingling with and walking among the great and the famous on equal terms, or within shuddering distance of the felons in the Separate Room. A contemporary Almanack, *Colburn's Calendar of Amusements*, called the exhibition 'one of the most delightful sights in London,' while remarking that, 'the first people of the day (past and present) appear as if attracted by the hospitality of Madame.' The same point was made by the magazine *Punch* which called her 'one of the national ornaments of the feminine species'. She enjoyed her royal patronage and prestige, but never forgot that it was ordinary people who made up the crowds mingling with her figures.

While success was bringing all its rewards after years of hard work,

Marie's domestic calm was disturbed in a most unexpected manner. Her husband, François Tussaud suddenly broke into her life again. She had not seen him since she left Paris on that November day in 1802, nor had direct contact with him since she wrote in 1804 that she was not going to return to Paris, and that her English enterprise meant more to her than he did. No doubt her second son Francis had kept up some kind of relations, since he had lived with his father and grandmother during his first twenty years or so, but for Marie he had almost ceased to exist, like all her French property that she had made over to him by power of attorney before she left the Lyceum Theatre all those years ago.

Now, in 1841, news of Madame Tussaud's fame and success in London seems to have reached François's ears in Paris. He felt that at seventy-two, and still living in the house that Curtius had built and left to Marie in the Rue Fossés du Temple, he should share in his wife's hard-earned prosperity.

On the pretext that he did not know the address of Madame Tussaud's exhibition in London, he took a first step of sending a letter to a friend, the Widow Castille, who was living there. He requested her to seek out his wife and show her this letter. Madame Castille did as she was asked and hastened to inform François, with a good deal of asperity, that her visit to Baker Street had not been well received.

Madame Tussaud, she wrote, had retained his letter in order to study it at her leisure. 'However,' went on Madame Veuve Castille, 'I must tell you, Sir, that she appears to hold against you some subjects of displeasure of considerable gravity for, from the first moment, she did not appear at all pleased to have news of you, and said she had given her sons all she possessed, as they were married to English ladies.'

She went on to point out tartly that Madame Tussaud had now lived in London for a number of years. A letter simply addressed to 'Madame Tussaud who owns a Salon of Figures' would have reached her as she was well known. There was no need to use an intermediary. The widow Castille then gave her opinion of Madame Tussaud's exhibition. 'It is impossible to describe the beauty and richness of her Salon. I have never in my life seen anything more magnificent. The entrance fee is a shilling per person, which is more than a French franc.'

Marie refused to have any direct contact with her husband. She was understandably incensed that he should approach her and seek to obtain some of the fruits of her work, skill, and determination. On 27 August, Joseph and Francis wrote a joint letter to their father at

No. 38 Rue Fossés du Temple. They wrote in rather clumsy French,

Monsieur,

Madame Tussaud and ourselves, not wishing to have any correspondence with you, believe that you have lived a sufficiently long time on support. Moreover having reached middle-age we believe this position and action is necessary. We hope, nonetheless, that Providence may do something for you, and that the Eternal God will be able to pardon your scandalous behaviour.

The exhibition is our property   F. Tussaud
                                                                    Joseph Tussaud

This uncompromising letter from his sons, following on Madame Castille's independent report of the hostility with which his hopeful 'feeler' had been received, deterred François from further action for the present, but he would return to the attack with more success three years later.

The distress and worry of her husband's attempted re-entry into her life thus shelved, Marie and her sons could concentrate on their next major project. The idea of setting up a memorial shrine to Napoleon Bonaparte had been germinating since the purchase of the Emperor's eagle battle standards at the sale of Waterloo spoils. More had been acquired from the estate of Prince Lucien, a younger brother of Napoleon, who had died in 1840. The concept of special Napoleon Rooms was now rapidly developing and they were to prove the apotheosis of Marie's personal career.

Though Napoleon had died in exile on the island of St Helena in 1821 he remained an object of peculiar fascination and interest to the British public. Marie herself had felt a kind of admiration for him since she modelled him as First Consul all those years ago at the request of his wife Josephine, and her last glimpse of the fallen hero on board ship in Torbay in 1815, on his way to exile. The Coronation of Napoleon tableau had always been a success, but was now outmoded in the enhanced exhibition in Bazaar.

Ledger entries during 1841 and 1842 record a series of purchases of Napoleonic relics. These included his camp bedstead, the cloak he wore at the battle of Marengo, a whip he had used, personal clothing and 'the mantles of Napoleon and Josephine'. The most important buy, however, was Napoleon's travelling carriage, which he had used at the battle of Waterloo.

After its capture on the battlefield the coach was presented to the Prince Regent (later George IV), and subsequently sold to a Mr Bullock who exhibited it from 1816 in the Egyptian Hall, Piccadilly, where it drew large crowds. Then it was taken on tour for some time, with equal success. It was said that as many as 900,000 people had seen it. The historic coach was then sold again with a view to exhibiting it in the United States, but the plan fell through. It changed hands several times, finally going in part payment of a debt to Robert Jeffreys, a coachbuilder in Gray's Inn Road. There it remained in obscurity for a long time, forgotten. No doubt it was in this carriage repository that Marie first noticed the dirty and cobwebbed relic and realised its potential in a proper setting. During the week ending 23 January 1842 her ledger records its purchase. The Prince Regent had sold it for £2,500. Marie paid £52 but a great deal of money and labour had to be spent restoring the coach to pristine condition.

It was obvious that special arrangements must be made for displaying this large Napoleonic collection. Other groups had been added to those already set up, such as the Armour Group of historical portraits, including Joan of Arc, and a tableau of Mary Queen of Scots being rebuked by John Knox. In addition to the tableaux and groups there were 43 single figures covering the spectrum of politics, history, the military, literature, and the stage, as well as English and French Royalty. The Separate Room had expanded with new likenesses of murderers and felons. In this year, 1842, Marie also modelled a new self-portrait. She was 81, much thinner than when her silhouette portrait was made, tiny, clad in a black dress and bonnet. Her eyes and her attitude were as alert as ever. Fortunately extra premises were available and in March 1843 the new rooms were ready. A special additional Catalogue was printed. The two rooms were described as being 'effected at a cost to the proprietors of £5,000. Magnificently fitted up after the designs of Isabey and Pountain, the Emperor's artists, forming a set of *National Reminiscences* of great interest, declared at the Public Office in the Court of Chancery, Southampton Buildings, before the following Masters: J. W. Farrer Esq., A. H. Lynch Esq., and Sir G. Wilson.' Marie was taking no chances that someone could question the authenticity of the historical relics she was displaying.

The ceilings were particularly splendid and great care was taken with picture frames which were made expressly to show 'the peculiar fashion of Napoleon's time'. The first, or Golden Room, known as the 'Shrine of Napoleon', had a figure of Napoleon 'from the best authority, David,' wearing clothing he had had at St Helena. These garments were from the estate of Prince Lucien Bonaparte. The many relics included 'the cradle of Napoleon's son, the King of Rome,' who had died in 1832 at the age of twenty-one. There was a wax model of a baby in the cradle, the likeness taken from a picture of the child by Gérard. In the second room the centrepiece was the Waterloo carriage, and the Splendid Table of Marshals which was on loan and for sale at the price of 4,000 guineas.

Admission to the Shrine of Napoleon and the Waterloo carriage room was 6d. The 'altogether matchless' exhibition, as Marie called it, was open from eleven in the morning till dusk, and then again from seven to ten in the evening.

The Napoleonic Rooms were an instant success and no-one queried the authenticity of the relics which had been so carefully documented and attested. Indeed nothing like it had been seen in London. Marie could at last feel that she had fulfilled the promise she made when she broke from her husband, to give her sons a good start in life. They were now middle-aged. Old though Marie was she had retained all her faculties to enjoy her victory over circumstances.

While the Napoleon Rooms were attracting crowds and money in London, François Tussaud, in Paris, still felt entitled to a share of this prosperity. He used his power of attorney over Marie's French property to chase a nebulous inheritance that Curtius had long ago claimed was due to him. Marie had never concerned herself with it, and after François had wasted time and money consulting lawyers he was persuaded that his quest was useless, as he could not produce the necessary documentation. So he turned his attention again to his wife and family in London, pleading old age (he was eight years younger than Marie), infirmity, and incapacity to manage his own affairs. This time he met with more success. His sons wrote that they now felt it was their duty to help him and they would journey to Paris to see what could be done. A postscript to their letter suggested they suspected their father of irresponsibility. 'N.B.' they added, 'Send reply to say that you will be in Paris.'

Marie acquiesced in this rapprochement, but refused to have any part in it herself. According to family tradition she forbade Joseph, who had left Paris with her at the age of four, actually to *see* his father. Francis of course, had already been a young man when he left the family home to join his mother in England. Joseph obeyed his mother till his curiosity overcame him. He went with Francis to the house in the Rue Fossés du Temple and, without being detected, peeped over a screen at his father. He saw no monster, but a harmless-looking old gentleman sitting in his chair.

Whatever arrangements were made, they evidently did not work out, for in September the brothers were again writing angrily to their father: 'Since you have enjoyed a life-interest in our mother's property, and she has received no profit from this property for so many years, she can in no way grant what you are seeking of her, seeing that, as we have already told you, this would naturally harm our interests. Therefore enjoy the life-interest as you please for the rest of your days.' A postscript again indicates François's weakness for a property gamble that was one of the original causes of dispute between Marie and her husband. 'Have the goodness to tell Monsieur Laurier, if he calls on you, that we have no wish whatsoever to enter into a speculation regarding a theatre.'

Troubled and alarmed by her husband's persistent attempts to get hold of a share in the exhibition, Marie consulted her '*homme d'affaires*' in London. From him she received full support in her refusal to accede to François Tussaud's demands. However, she was sole owner of her enterprise and under French law she could be vulnerable. Also he was considerably younger and might be able to claim the exhibition if she died first. On 3 July 1844, Articles of Partnership between Madame Marie Tussaud and her sons were signed. It was forty years since Marie had bought herself out of partnership with Philipstal. Since then, she, and she alone, had owned her exhibition. Now, at last, she had to cede her independence, but only to her two sons Joseph and Francis. She had been shaken by her husband's threats. As they wrote to their recalcitrant father, 'Every time you write to our mother she becomes very ill and especially when you write that you are coming to visit her, and that you are speaking in your position as husband. This is totally ridiculous.'

In spite of domestic anxieties the exhibition did not stand still. No matter how harassed she might be, work came first with Marie. New attractions included a group of Victoria and Prince Albert offering honours to the Duke of Wellington. Marie was able to state in the Catalogue that firms who advertised in it could be assured of a yearly circulation of at least 8,000 copies. A scenic ice attraction, with Glaciarium, which occupied the ground floor of Bazaar below Madame Tussaud's exhibition, moved away to Tottenham Court Road at the end of its lease, but the enlarged and much more hygienic and comfortable Cattle Show area brought increasing numbers of visitors, particularly as Queen Victoria had visited it herself with Prince Albert.

At Eastertime in 1844 Marie received the first of many mentions on the theatre stage. The Theatre Royal, Haymarket, was presenting *The Drama at Home* written by James Robinson Planche. The characters appearing in it included an impersonation of Madame Tussaud and two of her most colourful subjects, Commissioner Lin, who had been

commanded by the Emperor of China to prevent the spread of the
opium trade, and his wife, both eye-catchers in the 'magnificent
clothes work at the Court of Pekin'.

> To see you in clover comes Madame Tussaud
> Your model in waxwork she wishes to show
> The King of the French and Fieschi the traitor
> Commissioner Lin and the Great Agitator [Daniel O'Connell]
> Kings Princes, and Ministers all of them go
> To sit for their portraits to Madame Tussaud

The great circus showman P. T. Barnum, visiting London, was so
impressed by the Kings, Princes, Ministers, and other celebrities
gathered in the superb décor of the exhibition that he wanted to buy
the entire outfit and transport it to New York. His offer was rejected.
Marie had no intention of leaving London.

The following year, 1845, Marie's portrait in pastel was executed by
John George Paul Fischer. This artist had arrived in London from
Hanover to make his fortune eight years after Marie herself had
arrived. His Hanoverian connections gave him entrée to the Court,
where he painted miniature portraits of Queen Charlotte and her
family and a series depicting military costumes for the Prince Regent.
He painted the then Princess Victoria twice, first as an infant, then as
a child. A consistent exhibitor at the Royal Academy Paul Fischer was
now fifty-nine and he chose to paint his now celebrated subject sitting
at the entrance to the main hall of her exhibition, at a desk. Some
years after Marie's death, *Eyewitness* wrote a description of her in
Charles Dickens's periodical *All the Years Round* which confirmed the
accuracy of Fischer's portrayal: 'The present writer remembers her
well, sitting at the entrance of her own show and receiving the
shillings that poured into her Exchequer. She was evidently a person
of marked ability and of a shrewd and strong character.' Behind the
wrinkles, the spectacles, and the large bonnet was still evident the
cool, competent, young woman who inherited her 'uncle' Curtius's
exhibition, came to England to retrieve her finances single-handed,
managed to buy out her unsatisfactory partner Philipstal, and finally
took the decision to abandon her husband in order to forge a future
for her sons.

In spite of her advanced age Marie's skill and artistry as a sculptor in
wax was not failing. An article in the *Illustrated London News* commented on the 'air of life' that characterized her portrait figures and
remarked that a visit to Madame Tussaud's was 'next door to a
personal introduction to the famous'. Among those whom the visitor

MADAME TUSSAUD & SONS'
EXHIBITION,
BAZAAR, BAKER STREET, PORTMAN SQUARE.

The Author of the Chinese War!

The Destroyer of £2,500,000. of British Property, and his Small Footed Wife, the only Figures of the kind ever Exhibited in this Country.

COMMISSIONER LIN,
And his Favourite Consort,

Modelled from Life, by the Celebrated LAMB-QUA, of Canton, with the Magnificent Dresses actually worn by them, and the various Ornaments, &c.

Giving a perfect idea of the *Countenance, Costume, and Ornaments* of those singular people the Chinese, of whom so little is known ; lately brought to this Country by a Gentleman, a resident of Canton Eighteen Years, and to whom reference can be given.

Commissioner Lin was a notorious figure in the Opium War. In 1842 the addition of exotic figures of Lin and his wife drew crowds to the exhibition. *Madame Tussaud's Archives.*

could meet were 'The Royal Family at Home' in a new group, with the portraits modelled by Francis, while Joseph's wife was responsible for the costumes. A Hall of Kings was also beginning to take shape with new portraits of William III and James II.

Throughout 1845 François Tussaud in Paris continued to plague his family with requests for help, while failing to answer letters they sent to him. He was suffering from eye and leg trouble, and was already receiving some assistance from his sons. Of these Francis was the most sympathetic, understandably in view of his much closer relations with his father, and also perhaps due to a slight jealousy of his elder brother. He felt Joseph was his mother's favourite, though there is no evidence that Marie ever discriminated between her sons. Both were talented sculptors in wax.

It was in 1846 that the Separate Room acquired a new name that was to become a household word. The magazine *Punch* dubbed it the Chamber of Horrors in somewhat unusual circumstances. For the 'season' of 1846 Marie offered a special attraction:

'A Magnificent Display of Court Dresses of surpassing richness, comprising 25 ladies' and gentlemen's costumes intended to convey to the MIDDLE CLASSES an idea of the ROYAL SPLENDOUR, a most splendid novelty and calculated to display to young persons much necessary instruction.'

The editor of *Punch*, which had a considerable 'middle class' readership, saw the announcement and was exceedingly annoyed at its snobbish and somewhat patronising tone. It was the year of the repeal of the Corn Laws following on the disastrous harvest of 1845 in England and Ireland which brought hunger and misery to the poor. Under the headline 'A Great Moral Lesson at Madame Tussaud's' an article trounced her for this lavish display and finished:

The Collection should include specimens of the Irish peasantry, the hand-loom weavers, and other starving portions of the population all in their characteristic tatters; and also the inmates of the various workhouses in the ignominious garb presented for them by the Poor Law. But this department of the exhibition should be contained in a separate Chamber of Horrors and half a guinea entrance fee should be charged for the benefit of the living originals.

The new name caught the public imagination and became synonymous with the Separate Room.

Marie received more sarcastic publicity from *Punch* when, with her unerring sense of what was newsworthy, she represented among her portrait figures some clergy whose doctrinal disputes were highly

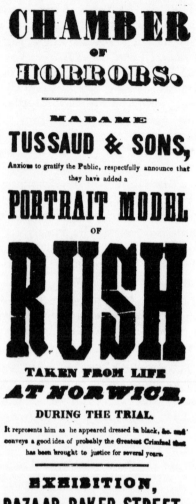

CHAMBER
OF
HORRORS.

MADAME
TUSSAUD & SONS,

Anxious to gratify the Public, respectfully announce that they have added a

PORTRAIT MODEL
OF

RUSH

TAKEN FROM LIFE
AT NORWICH,
DURING THE TRIAL.

It represents him as he appeared dressed in black, &c. and conveys a good idea of probably the Greatest Criminal that has been brought to justice for several years.

EXHIBITION,
BAZAAR, BAKER STREET,
Portman Square.

ADMITTANCE - ONE SHILLING.
CHAMBER of HORRORS, 6d.
Open from 11 in the Morning till 10 o'clock at Night.

J. W. PEEL's Steam Machine, 14, New Cut, Lambeth

James Blomfield Rush, a Norfolk farmer, was hanged in April 1849 for shooting landowner Mr Isaac Jermy and his son against whom he had a grievance over tenancy. *Madame Tussaud's Archives.*

topical. *Punch* mocked this in a fashion which, however scornful, brought in more interested visitors:

> Madame Tussaud presents her grateful compliments to a discerning public having had peculiar success with her CHAMBER OF HOR-RORS – a charming apartment cut off from the public room – in which are grouped together bloodshed and homicide in every variety. She has determined to set aside another nook in which the harmless eccentricities of various members of the Church may be duly commemorated. Madame Tussaud proposes to call the apart-ment 'Clerical Corner'.

The Chamber of Horrors not only satisfied the Victorian taste for the macabre, it became fashionable. The whole exhibition was fashionable. Cartoonists recognised it as an excellent subject. Cruik-shank's *I dreamt I slept at Madame Tussaud's* appeared in the *Comic Almanac* of 1847 and another famous cartoon, *A Row amongst the*

Cartoon by George Cruickshank from 'The Comic Almanack' for 1847.

> I dreamt that I slept at Madame Tussaud's
> With cut-throats and Kings side by side:
> And that all the wax figures in those abodes
> At midnight became revivified
> I dreamt that Napoleon Bonaparte
> Was waltzing with Madame Tee . . .

Madame Tussaud's Archives.

THE CHAMBER OF HORRORS.

WHILE every other branch of MADAME TUSSAUD's Exhibition is being enriched by "magnificent additions," it is a startling fact that the Chamber of Horrors has remained *in statu quo* for a considerable period. It is true, we have not lately had any FIESCHIS, with their infernal machines, or HARES and BURKES with their cold-blooded atrocities, to furnish subjects for this department of the interesting collection of MADAME TUSSAUD; we think, however, the enterprising and ingenious proprietor might meet with a new set of horrors in the present day, quite fit to take their place beside the darker horrors of an earlier period.

There are other tortures besides those of which her chamber fur-

nishes so many wondrous specimens. Where, for instance, could a finer subject be found for a Chamber of Horrors than the illustrious *Punch* in the excruciating agony of endeavouring to elucidate a joke just received from a Scotch humourist? Those only who know what it is to endure the infliction of a bit of alleged fun, reeking hot from Auld Reekie, may form some conception of the tortures endured by *Punch* in opening a letter, and finding it to contain a Caledonian witticism. Surely this would afford a powerful subject for a "magnificent addition" to MADAME TUSSAUD's Chamber of Horrors. The miseries of official life are also wonderfully suggestive of figures for the same portion of the Baker Street Wax-work. What

a picture of highly wrought wretchedness could be produced by a figure of a Government clerk, when, having read through the newspaper, he finds his day's "occupation gone," and delivering himself up to the torments of *ennui*, he becomes a prey to horrors of the most desolating description! How magnificent would be the effect of one harrowing blank delineated faithfully in the features of the melancholy object, who might be supposed to sigh in vain for one official note to write, one official envelope to open! If this is not a subject for the Chamber of Horrors, where shall we look for matter worthy of filling that gloomy apartment? But to go higher in the scale of official existence, we may find in the career of the Premier himself

sufficient subject for the Chamber we have been alluding to. Fancy the agony of poor LORD JOHN RUSSELL at the moment of being persecuted by a deputation, asking him for the hundred - and - ninetieth time the perplexing question, What is to be done with Ireland? We are sure that the active MADAME T. will take our hint, and supply the omissions in her Chamber of Horrors as speedily as possible.

A SITE AT LAST.

AT length the Wellington Statue will be placed on a site that must satisfy the grumblers. In the very handsomest manner, a piece of ground has been allotted to it in their own property, by the proprietors of the Thames Tunnel.

The magazine *Punch* had a continuing interest in the Chamber of Horrors. Article published in 1847. *Madame Tussaud's Archives.*

Figures, illustrated a popular song about a midnight political fracas among the 'waxy lot'.

Marie Tussaud lived and died a French citizen, but in 1847 her sons, both French-born, applied for 'denization'. Joseph was living at No. 58 Baker Street, while Francis had his home nearby at 18 Salisbury Place, New Road (now a part of Marylebone Road). One of the sponsors for this naturalization process was Admiral Napier, who had been elected Member of Parliament for Marylebone in 1840. He had had a famous naval career and his portrait figure stood in the exhibition. Since Joseph had come to England at the age of four, and Francis had lived in the country for over twenty years this was a sensible step. But it also had practical advantages. Both sons were now co-proprietors of the exhibition with their mother. Their father, in spite of age and infirmity, was still angling for a share in the enterprise. If Marie predeceased him, and all three proprietors were French, problems could arise with French law.

Up to this point Marie's mental and physical vigour had remained remarkable, though Francis wrote to his father in Paris that she seemed to grow thinner every day. Her grandchildren remembered her vitality. One of them was Joseph Randall, eldest son of Francis. He entered the Royal Academy Schools and trained under the sculptor Sir Richard Westmacott, in due course to take over from his father in the exhibition. Joseph Randall, many years later, recalled his grandmother:

> I remember my grandmother perfectly, although I was quite a young man at the time she died in 1850. Up to within three years of her death she was a very familiar figure in the exhibition. I can see her now, very small and slight, and wearing a bandana handkerchief tied about her head after the manner of French women in full dress to keep her hair tidy. Her eyes were vivacious and she was a great talker, full of anecdotes and blessed with a faultless memory. She was a Catholic, but during the greater part of her life piety was not one of her characteristics. She was 'converted' at the end by a religious relative, and passed a good deal of her time in prayer and meditation but to the horror of her pious companion she generally used a large crucifix which had been placed in her room as a cap-stand. She used to say 'Beware my children, of the three black crows – the doctor, the lawyer, and the priest.' She was always very charitable and generous to a fault, but she was decidedly a character.

Now, at last, age was catching up with her. Marie began to suffer with asthma which gave her no rest at night. Periodically she became really ill, and her legs, which had danced so energetically on the ruins of the Bastille in Paris in 1789 were giving trouble.

However, Marie's husband François was to predecease her in spite of her eight years' seniority. Her ban on Joseph actually having contact with his father had been lifted, and the acrimony between François and his sons had died down. His death was not expected. In the autumn of 1848 Joseph went to Paris to visit his father. In a letter written in October he agreed, with his brother, to pay half of the rent of an apartment into which François wished to move, away from the Rue Fossés du Temple. He appeared to be in reasonably good health for his age, and was looked after by a widow in the capacity of 'dame de compagnie'. When he wrote Joseph sent his compliments to this Madame Bertrand, and thanked her for the care she took of his father.

François's health deteriorated and, on 12 November, feeling his end was near, he made a will, leaving 500 francs to Madame Bertrand as recompense for her care, and once this had been paid, any of his remaining possessions she might wish to take. 'This is the free expression of my last wish,' he dictated and tried to sign his will. He was too blind to do so. However, a lawyer and witnesses were present so the will was completed. It made no mention of the wife he had said goodbye to 46 years ago, and whose property had supported him ever since. Four days after making his will François died and the funeral took place in the Church of St Elizabeth, Rue du Temple. He had never left the district in which he had met and married Marie Grosholtz. A computation of rights made after the funeral showed that little was left of the dowry Marie had brought to her marriage. The famous exhibition, the *Salon de Cire* in the Boulevard du Temple had been long since ceded to meet mortgage payments, and house property sold. All Marie's links with her old life in Paris were now severed.

Sixteen months later, on 15 April 1850, Marie herself died peacefully. She left everything to her sons and her last enjoinder to them was 'Do not quarrel'. She was in her 90th year, and was buried in the churchyard of the Roman Catholic Chapel in Chelsea, which had been a centre and refuge for many émigrés of the French Revolution.

At the end of the century a new Catholic Church of St Mary was built in Chelsea not far from the site of the Chapel which was closed. The coffins buried in its churchyard were removed and sealed into the crypt of the new Church. Marie's bones lie there, and in the Church a memorial tablet records her death and those of some of her descendants. Madame Tussaud had become internationally known and obituary notices appeared in many newspapers and periodicals.

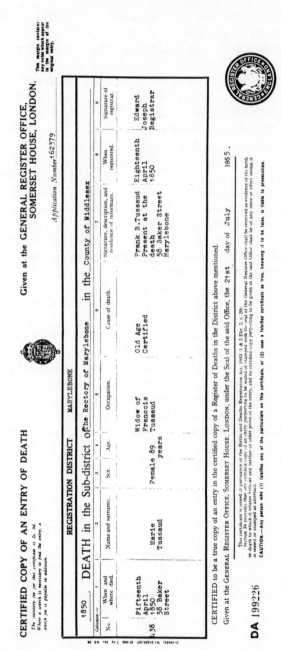

Marie Tussaud's death certificate.

Perhaps Marie would have enjoyed best what Thackeray wrote in the month she died. Under the pseudonymn Goliath Muff he said in his *Sights of London*, 'I have only to say that rather than be left alone in *that* Gallery at night with those statues, I would consent to be locked up with one of the horrid lions in the Zoological Gardens.'

A pioneer career woman, though she never considered herself remotely in any such context, Marie died in the knowledge that she had accomplished everything she determined to do after her 'uncle' Curtius's death, despite her marriage that proved so unsatisfactory and her one disastrous venture into partnership. From the day she broke with Philipstal in Dublin in 1804, she was self-sufficient. She left her sons a splendid exhibition of international celebrity, and earned herself prestige and respect both as an artist and a business woman.

What drove her on? What sustained her throughout her long, extraordinary, and often hard and difficult life? It was not a desire for money as such. The exhibition might be sumptuous, but Marie's lifestyle remained simple. She made no attempt, as success came, to acquire grand houses, jewels, fine clothes or objets d'art. She met the highborn, the wealthy, and the famous, but had no wish to enter Society, to entertain or be entertained.

Marie was, by all accounts, vivacious, voluble, full of anecdotes, with a French woman's aplomb. 'Everyone' knew Madame Tussaud. At the same time no one knew Marie. She revealed nothing of her personal emotions, her personal feelings. What had she really felt at Versailles, and during the terrible Revolutionary years? Did she ever despair as she travelled the length and breadth of a foreign land? She confided in no-one, not even her sons. As a person she remains an enigma. The one thing that is certain is that her English 'enterprise' succeeded far beyond what she could ever have imagined.

CHAPTER VI

The Descendants

AS she would have wished it, Marie's death was not allowed to disrupt the exhibition. The loss of this remarkable woman, who had been firmly in control almost until her last breath, left a grief and a void felt by all those who had worked for her, many for years. However, as Marie would have declared, the shop must be taken care of, and there was important work ahead.

In March 1850, a month before Marie's death, a Royal Commission, with Prince Albert as its Chairman, had been set up to finalise and approve plans for a Great Exhibition to be staged in London in 1851. This would be in Hyde Park and housed in the vast structure of glass and iron, covering sixteen acres, that came to be known as the Crystal Palace. It was a project designed to bring visitors from all over the world flocking into the capital. Many of them would also pay a visit to Madame Tussaud's exhibition.

Joseph and Francis were already at work on a new addition to be created in honour of Prince Albert with whom the idea of the Great Exhibition had originated. This addition had certainly been discussed with and approved by Marie who retained her faculties to the end. There was to be a new Hall of Kings, covering the spectrum of English monarchy from early times to Queen Victoria. Such a scheme required space, and space was now available at Bazaar, Baker Street, in the form of a vast room 243 feet long by 48 feet wide and ideal for the 'uninterrupted vista' required.

The new Gallery would, like Curtius's original *Salon de Cire* in Paris, combine portrait figures of the Kings and Queens of England with pictures and sculpture. Paintings already acquired included Queen Victoria in her Coronation robes by Hayter, William IV by Simpson, King George III and Queen Charlotte as depicted by Reynolds, George II portrayed by Hudson, a copy of Lawrence's famous painting of King George IV in his robes, and a picture of the Prince Consort by Patten. The cost of setting up the Hall of Kings was extremely high, but it was all re-couped within a year by proceeds from the influx of extra visitors who came to see the Great Exhibition which opened in May 1851 and included Madame Tussaud's exhibition in their sightseeing.

In this project Joseph and Francis confirmed that they intended to build on the three foundation stones of their late mother's policy; spectacle, ever updated coverage of who and what was in the news and educational value. Nor were her *coup d'oeil* and lighting forgotten. By 1860 the vistas of the exhibition were illuminated by five hundred lamps.

Marie had made secure her sons' tenure of the exhibition but in due course arrangements had to be made to ensure the family succession. Neither Joseph nor his family inherited the robust longevity of his mother. His daughter Mary died in 1847. Eleven years later he lost his only son Francis Babbington, a trained and talented sculptor, who sadly died in Rome at the age of twenty-nine having gone to a warm climate for his health. Joseph had one daughter left Louisa Elizabeth, who married a Doctor of Philosophy, W. D. Kenny.

In 1864, therefore, and only a year before his own death at the age of sixty-seven, Joseph entered into a deed of partnership with his brother Francis, his daughter Louisa Kenny, and Joseph Randall, the eldest of Francis's three sons. In due course Joseph Randall would take over control of the exhibition. Louisa does not appear to have had any talent or training in sculpture but worked in the wardrobe and kept the ledgers. When the time came to take over Joseph Randall also had the assistance of his two brothers, Victor and Francis Curtius, who lived to be ninety like his grandmother.

Louisa Kenny, now a partner and her father's principal legatee when he died in 1867, was to cause problems. Tiring of her doctor of philosophy husband she formed a liaison with a French Marquis de Leuville. In the end she was able to marry him, but before that she caused scandal by going to live with the Marquis in the South of France. There, in Nice, she had a carriage and pair and used to drive along the promenade in the fashionable parade. Her lifestyle required money which the Marquis evidently could not provide. Louisa withdrew her share of capital from the partnership, causing her cousins financial embarrassment. A precious Boucher painting in the exhibition had to be sold. Unlike her grandmother Marie, Louisa did not put work and the exhibition first. However, she died in the South of France as the Marquise de Leuville thus attaining the status of 'great lady' which had once been attributed to her grandmother in Edinburgh, where she had friends in the Castle, long ago in 1803.

Dr Philippe Curtius wearing his National Guard uniform, by Gilles Louis Chrétien, circa 1790. *Bibliothèque Nationale, Paris.*

Portrait of Madame Tussaud in middle age by an unknown artist. *Madame Tussaud's Archives.*

Portrait bust of Francis Tussaud, Marie Tussaud's second son, born in 1800; believed to be by his son Joseph Randall. *Madame Tussaud's Archives.*

Portrait of Joseph Tussaud, Marie Tussaud's elder son, born in 1798, by an unknown artist. *Madame Tussaud's Archives.*

A family group of silhouettes by Joseph Tussaud. His mother is on the left, a self-portrait on the right, and his wife, Elizabeth Babbington at the harp. *Madame Tussaud's Archives.*

Edinburgh in 1803 when Madame Tussaud paid her first visit. Waterloo Place by Thomas Shepherd. *Edinburgh Public Libraries.*

The Grand Assembly Room, York, a typical venue for showing Madáme Tussaud's wax portrait figures. Engraving by William Lindley. *City Art Gallery, York.*

The Bristol Riots, 1831. Mobs set fire to the north side of Queen's Square, endangering Madame Tussaud's exhibition. William Muller, eyewitness, made a water-colour drawing showing her figures being carried out of the Assembly Rooms. *Madame Tussaud's Archives.*

'The Green Man', Blackheath, in whose spacious rooms Madame Tussaud set up her exhibition in 1833. *Madame Tussaud's Archives.*

The Market Place, Hull, visited by Madame Tussaud in 1826. The carriage and wagon are the type used by her on her travels. From *The Penny Magazine* 13 September 1834. *Madame Tussaud's Archives.*

Tableau of George IV in his Coronation robes in the Great Room
at Madame Tussaud's exhibition, Baker Street. From Mead's *London
Interiors*, 1840. *Madame Tussaud's Archives.*

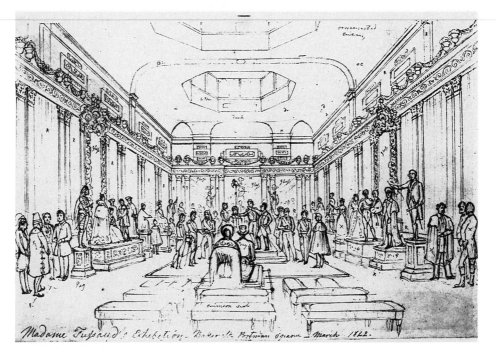

Sketch showing seating in the Great Room of Madame Tussaud's exhibition, Baker Street, in 1842. She wished visitors to be able to study the
groups and figures as well as promenading round. *Madame Tussaud's
Archives.*

Vista of the Great Room of Madame Tussaud's exhibition at Bazaar, Baker Street. It was elaborately decorated and was claimed to be the largest public room in Europe. *Madame Tussaud's Archives.*

Mr. Pips his Diary.

Wednesday, September 5, 1849.—To please my Wife, did take her this Evening to MADAME TUSSAUD her Wax Works; a grand large Room, exceeding fine with Gilding, lighted up very splendid, and full of People, and a Band of Musique playing as they walked about: cost 2s., and a Catalogue 6d. The Wax Figures a pretty Show: but with their painted Cheeks and glassy Eyes—especially such as nod and move—do look like Life in Death. The Dresses very handsome, and I think, correct; and the Sight of so many People of Note in the Array of their Time, did much delight me. Among the Company Numbers of Country Folk, and to see how they did stare at the Effigies of the QUEEN, and the PRINCE, and the DUKE OF WELLINGTON, and the KING OF THE BELGIANS, and the PRINCESS CHARLOTTE that was, and GEORGE THE FOURTH in his Coronation Robes, magnificent as a Peacock! The Catalogue do say that his Chair is the very one wherein he sat in the Abbey; but how like a Play-House Property it do look, and little thought the King it would come down to figure in a Raree Show! A Crowd of Dames and Matrons gazing at the Group of the Royal Family, calling the Children "D^rars" and "Ducks," and would, I verily believe, have kissed their Wax Chaps, if they had been suffered. My Wife feasting her Eyes on the little Princes and Princesses, I did fix mine upon a pretty, modest, black Maid beside me, and she hers on me, till my Wife spying us, did pinch me with her Nails in the Arm. Pretty, to see the Sovereign Allies in the last War, and bluff old BLUCHER, and BONAPARTE and his Officers, in brave Postures, but stiff. Also the two KING CHARLESES, and OLIVER, together; CHARLES THE FIRST protesting against his Death-Warrant,

and his Son backing him; and CARDINAL WOLSEY looking on. LORD BYRON in the Dress of a Greek Pirate, looking Daggers and Pistols, close to JOHN WESLEY preaching a Sermon, was likewise mighty droll; and methought, if all MADAME TUSSAUD'S Figures were their Originals instead, what Ado there would be! Many of the Faces that I knew by Recollection, or Pictures, very like; and my LORD BROUGHAM I did know directly, and LISTON in *Paul Pry*. But strange, among the Kings to see him that was the Railway King; and methinks that it were as well now if he were melted up. Thence to the NAPOLEON Rooms, where BONAPARTE'S Coach, and one of his Teeth, and other Reliques and Gimcracks of his, well enough to see for such as care about him a Button. Then to the Chamber of Horrors, which my Wife did long to see most of all; cost, with the NAPOLEON Rooms, 1s. more; a Room like a Dungeon, where the Head of ROBESPIERRE, and other Scoundrels of the great French Revolution, in Wax, as though just cut off, horrid ghastly, and Plaster Casts of Fellows that have been hanged: but the chief Attraction a Sort of Dock, wherein all the notorious Murderers of late Years; the foremost of all, RUSH, according to the Bill, taken from Life at Norwich, which, seeing he was hanged there, is an odd Phrase. There was likewise a Model of Stanfield Hall, and RUSH his Farm, as though the Place were as famous as Waterloo. Methinks it is of ill Consequence that there should be a Murderers' Corner, wherein a Villain may look to have his Figure put more certainly than a Poet can to a Statue in the Abbey. So away again to the large Room, to look at JENNY LIND instead of GREENACRE, and at 10 of the Clock Home, and so to Bed, my Wife declaring she should dream of the Chamber of Horrors.

Printed by William Bradbury, of No. 13, Upper Woburn-place, in the Parish of St. Pancras, and Frederick Mullet Evans, of No. 7, Church-row, Stoke Newington, both in the County of Middlesex, Printers, at their Office, in Lombard-street, in the Precinct of Whitefriars, in the City of London, and published by them at No. 85 Fleet-street, in the Parish of St. Bride's, in the City of London.—SATURDAY, SEPTEMBER 15, 1849.

Cartoon and article from *Punch*, 15 September 1849. *Madame Tussaud's Archives.*

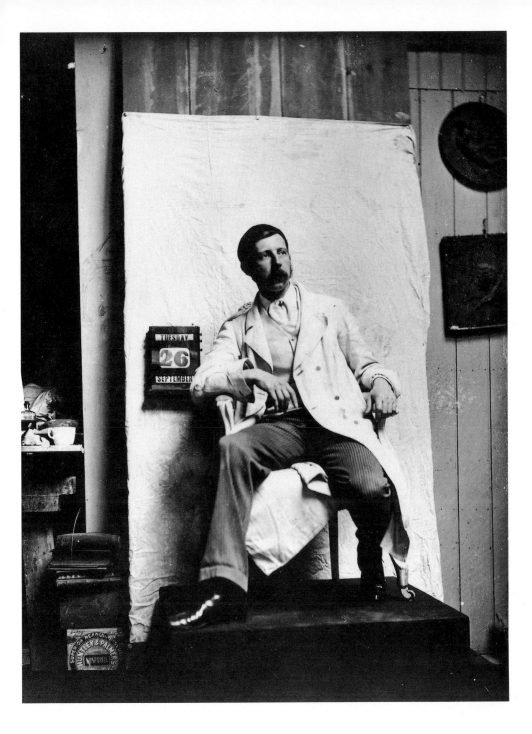

John Theodore Tussaud, great-grandson of Marie Tussaud, in his studio.
Photography was one of his many hobbies. *Madame Tussaud's Archives.*

The Napoleon Group, added to Madame Tussaud's exhibition in 1888. The figures include Napoleon Bonaparte, Napoleon III, Empress Euginie, and the Prince Imperial. *Madame Tussaud's Archives.*

One of John Theodore Tussaud's famous scenic tableaux, representing Commandant Cronje surrendering to Lord Roberts on 27 February 1900 during the Boer War. *Madame Tussaud's Archives.*

During the night of 18 March 1925 Madame Tussaud's premises in the
Marylebone road were almost completely destroyed by fire. *Madame
Tussaud's Archives*

Bernard Tussaud, great-great-grandson of Marie Tussaud, working on his portrait of Richard Dimbleby. *Madame Tussaud's Archives.*

John Theodore Tussaud, great-grandson of Marie Tussaud with members of his family. Three of his sons served in the First World War. *Madame Tussaud's Archives.*

On the night of 9/10 September 1940 a German bomb destroyed the cinema, a mould store, and badly damaged the restaurant of Madame Tussaud's. King George VI and Queen Elizabeth came to inspect the crater. *Madame Tussaud's Archives.*

Bernard Tussaud's portrait figure of Adolf Hitler often had to be repaired after attacks were made on it by members of the public. *Madame Tussaud's Archives.*

19 April 1959. Bernard Tussaud, great-great-grandson of Madame Tussaud, with his mother, aged 93, and staff of Madame Tussaud's exhibition. *Madame Tussaud's Archives.*

Bernard Tussaud, great-great-grandson of Marie Tussaud with her last self-portrait in wax. *Madame Tussaud's Archives.*

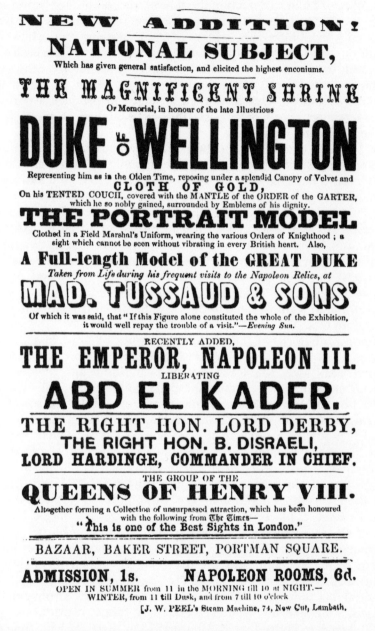

The Duke of Wellington, a regular patron of Madame Tussaud's exhibition, died in September 1852. By Christmas he was commemorated by 'a Magnificent Shrine' set up in the Great Room. *Madame Tussaud's Archives.*

In spite of Louisa's defection the flow of 'new additions' continued, both in the galleries and in the Chamber of Horrors. Madame Tussaud's exhibition was seldom caught napping but when the famous novelist Charles Dickens died suddenly in 1870 a crisis arose. Curiously the great writer who had so often mentioned the exhibition in his periodicals had never been modelled. When his death was announced Joseph Randall worked all night to produce a portrait, considered an excellent likeness though modelled at speed from photographs and pictures.

In 1872 the case of the Tichborne Claimant aroused much public interest. The Tichbornes were an ancient family and when Sir Alfred, the eleventh baronet, died an astonishing claim to be the heir came from a butcher from Wagga Wagga in Australia. He was impersonating a brother of the deceased baronet, who had been lost at sea off America. His case collapsed on the 103rd day of a trial to assert his claim, and he turned out to be one Arthur Orton from Wapping. Orton was then tried for perjury, another immensely long trial said to have cost the then enormous sum of £55,315. In the end Arthur Orton confessed his imposture and was sentenced to fourteen years imprisonment. Crowds came to the Chamber of Horrors to look at his portrait in wax.

Among other crowd pullers was the figure of Lord Mayo, assassinated Viceroy of India, which was so lifelike that his housekeeper fainted dead away when she saw it. Livingstone and Stanley, the African explorers, joined the ranks, the latter accompanied by his native boy Kalula. Royal connections continued. At the request of the Duchess of Teck (mother of Princesss May, later Queen Mary) Joseph Randall modelled a portrait of 'The Soldier's Wife', Dinah Kitcher who, like many another of her kind, had accompanied her husband on campaigns in many countries. The figure of Mrs Kitcher was first shown at a charity bazaar of which the Duchess of Teck was patron, but then became a feature of the exhibition, so popular that it actually held its place until 1931. The marriage of Princess Louise, one of Queen Victoria's daughters, to the Marquess of Lorne made a charming group in 1871. New Court dresses by the famous couturier Worth added glamour, and the dress which clothed the figure of Princess Alice was described in the Press as 'splendid'.

Advancing years were now catching up with Marie's younger son Francis, who, like his brother, lacked her robust constitution. His health began to fail and on 31 August 1873 he died. His wife, Rebecca Smallpage, was still alive, though ailing, and apart from the bevy of daughters there were his three sons Joseph Randall, Victor, and

Francis Curtius, already active in the exhibition. Francis's will, like that of his elder brother Joseph, was proved at 'under £40,000' and after provision for his wife and daughters the residue went to his sons. Francis died knowing that the succession was already secure. John Theodore, son of Joseph Randall, and born in 1858, had, like his great grandmother Marie, taken to wax modelling at an early age. He had first tried his hand at it when aged five, and already a portrait figure he had modelled stood in the exhibition.

On the death of his father Francis, Joseph Randall Tussaud became modeller-in-chief. A talented sculptor and possessed of considerable culture, he had, in early manhood, to battle with two enemies, adversaries that had never crossed Marie's path, but which her grandson might have inherited from her unsatisfactory husband. On 16 November 1870 Joseph Randall wrote in his diary: 'Having so far conquered the inclination to drunkenness as to refrain from exciting liquids as nearly as I can remember for seven weeks to the hour, I intend with my full strength of *will* to fight against my next besetting sin, *procrastination*.' Joseph Randall evidently possessed much of his grandmother's determination for there is no further record of these weaknesses.

The circle of Marie's descendants was much enlarged by Joseph Randall's family, for he had thirteen children. He was devoted to his wife Ellen, 'my Nellie' as he called her, but it should not be imagined she was a Victorian martyr to over-frequent pregnancies. She adored children, and was once observed crying after being told of the birth of another grandchild. Asked why this glad news had caused an outburst of grief, she replied that she was weeping for herself as she was past the age of producing more children.

The exhibition continued to flourish at Bazaar for another decade. There were many distinguished sitters, special lighting effects, such as illuminations on the Prince of Wales's birthday, with new groups and tableaux. Often there were special attractions, including a series 'Fashions of the Day' with dresses imported from Paris. This drew much attention in a day when only a comparative few were able to view high fashion at close quarters. Royal and aristocratic visitors continued to patronise the exhibition. The Kings of Sweden and Norway and the Grand Duke and Duchess of Teck were among them, as well as an exotic oriental couple known as the 'Marquis and Marchioness Tseng'.

Nevertheless the exhibition's days at Bazaar were numbered. There were problems with the landlords regarding renewal of the lease. The three Tussaud brothers, Marie's grandchildren Joseph Randall, Victor and Francis Curtius took a momentous decision. Firmly established as a London landmark, highly successful with international fame, and with a reservoir of young talent coming on in the family, the time had come when Madame Tussaud's exhibition could, for the first time since Marie landed in England in 1802, abandon leased premises for a purpose-built building of its own. A site was available in Marylebone Road, only a short distance from the location already familiar to thousands of visitors.

In 1882 excavations began on the new site, and a major purchase was made for the edifice that would arise there. This was 'Baron Grant's' famous marble staircase supported by marble caryatids. Baron Grant was a financial adventurer whose original name was Gottheimer. He received a barony from the King of Italy and at one time was MP for Kidderminster and owner of a newspaper, the *Echo*. He amassed an immense fortune as a company promoter, and in 1872 began laying out Leicester Square which he had acquired. After spending £20,000 in embellishment he presented Leicester Square as a gift to the nation in 1874. However lawsuits brought Baron Grant to bankruptcy. His magnificent mansion in Kensington was taken over by creditors, and was stripped of its fittings including its wonderful marble staircase. This had cost thousands of pounds but was purchased by the Tussaud brothers for £1,000. As for Baron Grant, he was soon forgotten, his gift of Leicester Square to the people overlooked, and he died in obscurity in Bognor in 1899. Another prestigious acquisition was a series of ceiling panels painted by Sir James Thornhill, a favourite artist of Queen Anne. His best known work was the ceiling he had painted at Greenwich Hospital.

The actual building of the new exhibition began early in 1883. The press reports during Marie's lifetime which used to say she never allowed anything 'cheap or got-up looking' were certainly true of the building erected by her grandsons in the Marylebone Road. The construction was of the most solid and substantial nature. Stone dormer windows were filled in with handsome frames and glass, and there was a balustrade in red concrete. Inside, the lofty hall rose to a dome of glass and iron and Baron Grant's two flight staircase had marble landings. The lower walls were panelled in coloured marbles, while the upper portions and roof cornice were painted plaster, picked out with gold. The upstairs halls were very fine too. The first, approached from a marble landing, had the ceiling panels filled in with the Thornhill paintings. Its walls were covered in drapery and there was a platform for the orchestra. The musical promenade, instituted by Marie during her travelling years, was still an important feature. The Grand Hall was very lofty, lit by two large domes, with the ceiling and cornice in ornamental plaster. In all there were seven halls including the Napoleon Rooms and the Chamber of Horrors, while a conservatory was a new attraction at the west end of the building. Even in its palmiest days Curtius's *Salon de Cire* at the Boulevard du Temple in Paris had never approached this grandeur.

Ironically, as the future was to prove, special care was taken with fire precautions. Marie had always dreaded fire since she fled the Lyceum Theatre on account of a gas-lighting exhibition when she was showing there in 1803. The floors of all seven halls were considered fireproof under the black oak flooring that covered them. Heating was by hot water pipes and main water laid on throughout to service the fire hydrants, five on each floor, in positions capable of covering the whole range with a hose, while two permanent firemen were employed. As a fire risk the surveyor considered the building to be 'first-class'. Marie's great-grandson, John Theodore, who was twenty-six when the work was finished, must have recalled all the precautions when, forty-one years on, he saw it all engulfed in flames.

The stupendous task of moving the 400 wax portrait figures and all the paraphernalia of the Bazaar exhibition took a week. The actual removal was carried out by the firm of Whiteley's. Exhausted workers stretched out to sleep between the sheeted wax figures laid out on the floor awaiting transportation to their palatial new home which was reputed to have cost £80,000.

On 14 July, the anniversary of the fall of the Bastille and beginning of the French Revolution, Madame Tussaud's exhibition re-opened. The preview was attended by many distinguished guests including a gaggle of peers and many MPs. The guests were regaled with champagne, ices, and strawberries and cream. The exhibition had come a long way since its début in the Lyceum theatre. Marie's steely determination to establish a success was fully justified in these halls, a perfect expression of contemporary Victorian taste. Press acclaim was universal. Further embellishments were quickly added, including an orchestra of lady instrumentalists playing throughout the day. One reporter commented with satisfaction that visitors exhausted with promenading and gazing could now refresh themselves with beer, wine, chops, and steaks, instead of only buns and tea.

Joseph Randall Tussaud, having accomplished this splendid monument to his grandmother Marie, now began to find the burden of running it too heavy. In 1885 he retired from his controlling position. Joseph Randall's health had never been very good. In his diary he frequently complained of colds and other ailments: 'infernal cold still on,' and 'I am evidently suffering from a great depression due to cold.' He had certainly not inherited Marie's unremitting drive, but his eldest son John Theodore, in his twenties, was already a forceful character and ready to step into his shoes. Another son, Louis, and a nephew, were also completing their training before joining the family business.

Joseph Randall died seven years after his retirement at the comparatively early age of sixty-one. His last years were marred by financial troubles and the death of his beloved wife Ellen. He had been a fine sculptor, exhibiting several times at the Royal Academy, as well as a cultured and book-loving man who liked to read aloud to his wife from his favourite authors, Thackeray amongst them.

During the years immediately following the opening of the new Marylebone Road building it became evident that the enterprise had become too large and too complex to continue as a purely family business. Up to the end of her life Marie had always refused to consider any outside participation. Her one short but stormy experience with Philipstal when she first came to England always remained fresh in her mind. But now things had to be different. In 1888, a year when 400,000 visitors passed through the turnstiles, Madame Tussaud's exhibition was registered as a limited company. The following year the necessary financial support was forthcoming. John Theodore Tussaud, Marie's great-grandson, was appointed chief artist and manager, a position that he held until his sudden death at the age of eighty-five in 1943. Five of Marie's descendants had signed the Article of Association.

Unfortunately the new organisation of the exhibition did not come into being without causing some of the family friction against which she had warned on her death bed: 'Do not quarrel', she had said. Louis Tussaud, brother of John Theodore, was not pleased with the lessened freedom that came inevitably when the business ceased to be an entirely family matter. He broke away, deciding to buy a site and create a new exhibition that would be entirely under his own control. He too was a trained and talented sculptor. Litigation followed and he was obliged to abandon this plan. Instead he set up a gallery of wax portrait figures in Regent Street, hoping to rival not only the exhibition in Marylebone Road, but also the Musée Grévin, the wax exhibition now set up in Paris. His hope was short-lived. Within a year Louis Tussaud's gallery was consumed by the fire that his great-grandmother had always dreaded. Thenceforward he was only active in a small way in the provinces, severing all connection with the family exhibition for which his father, Joseph Randall, had had him trained.

During the long reign of John Theodore Madame Tussaud's exhibition was to reach new pinnacles of fame, and to survive two world wars and a disastrous fire. John Theodore was a remarkable personality with an energy and drive as strong as that of his great-grandmother Marie. He inherited her artistic talent and sense of showmanship as well. A journal that he kept often notes 'spent the night at the exhibition' just as Marie and small Joseph had so frequently worked into the night while touring England, Ireland and Scotland. During his long life John Theodore modelled literally hundreds of portraits. His first, of King Milan, monarch of that troubled land Serbia, was placed in the exhibition when he was only fourteen years old. His work reflected contemporary history, and he was known to dozens of famous people from all walks of life and to many members of the British and foreign Royal families.

Unlike Marie, who never willingly plied her pen, her great-grandson wrote two books, one a history of the exhibition called *The Romance of Madame Tussaud* and the other about the Generals who accompanied Napoleon to exile in St Helena. Newspaper and magazine articles flowed from his pen. Riding, driving, sketching from nature, and portrait painting were among John Theodore's hobbies, the chief of which was an interest in mechanical engineering. He also devised a number of ingenious inventions, one of which was a special clay for modelling. Some of these devices were even patented.

John Theodore did not share his great-grandmother's temperament, for he was something of a martinet and had an irascible, often difficult, temper. His five sisters, who worked in the wardrobe and hair and colouring studios were seen to tremble if their brother entered with a look of displeasure on his face. Nor were his relations always harmonious with his brothers and his children, of whom he had ten. John Theodore's wife, whom he married in 1889, was a woman of considerable artistic talent, particularly skilled in fine needlework and embroidery.

Marie's great-grandson carried on all the traditions on which she had founded her success and made some special contributions of his own. One of these was the development of the tableaux for which the exhibition became famous worldwide in the period between Queen Victoria's death in 1901, and the First World War. The earliest of these scenic tableaux represented the sporting tastes of the period, 'The Boat Race', 'Cricket Match at Lords', 'Covert Shooting', 'Fishing', 'Yachting'. They conjured up the sporting/social occasions for which the Edwardian period was famous. The figures were realistically modelled by John Theodore, and the scenic backgrounds were by superior artists such as Bruce Smith. The popular 'Death of Nelson' tableau was first shown at the Naval Exhibition in 1891, and caused a noble visitor to exclaim, 'Why, it beats Tussaud's', not realising that it was indeed John Theodore's creation. Historical and literary subjects, explorers and war scenes followed, all reflecting public interest at the time, a sight no visitor to the capital could miss.

In this period the Chamber of Horrors also reached pinnacles of fame. On Boxing Day of 1891 a crowd of 31,000 people blocked the streets around, waiting to see the portrait figure of the murderess Mrs Pearcey, standing in her reconstructed sitting room, the furniture and other items of which had been purchased by John Theodore. It was in this Hampstead sitting room that Eleanor Pearcey battered to death the wife and baby of her secret lover Frank Hogg, when Mrs Hogg was paying a friendly visit. Mrs Pearcey then wheeled the corpses in the baby's perambulator to some waste ground. She was convicted and met her inevitable end on the scaffold. During her trial a reporter for the publication *Pioneer* wrote prophetically: 'She sat in the dock motionless as a waxwork in Madame Tussaud's.' There was also a series of small tableaux 'The Story of a Crime', designed to 'chill the blood and teach a moral lesson'. The Victorian taste for both the macabre and a moral lesson was well catered for in the Chamber of Horrors.

John Theodore, like Marie, knew the importance of lighting in presentation. In November 1880 the installation of electric lighting was completed. A party for 200 guests was held to celebrate the switch-on of this modern system of illumination and the opening of a new tableau, 'The Execution of Mary Queen of Scots', specially created for the occasion.

By 1900 more space was needed. Several houses alongside the building, which had been used as offices and shops, were pulled down so that the site could be used for a new restaurant and offices, while the space occupied by the old restaurant was used for more crowd-pulling tableaux. The first year of the new century saw the opening of the Dining Hall, an impressive salon in which 'much use has been made of fumigated [sic] oak, the centre buffet being a splendid piece of work; the comfortable chairs are covered with maroon morocco.' It was a perfect reflection of contemporary taste.

New heating also went in, the hot water system of 1884 being replaced by a new method of steam heat installed by the Atmospheric Steam Heating Co.

John Theodore's creative mind made him eager to profit from any new inventions. Music, first introduced by Marie while still travelling with the exhibition, had continued as an important extra attraction. A variety of orchestras and bands now played during opening hours. In 1908 a new musical attraction appeared to surprise and interest visitors. This was an 'auxetophone', worked by electricity. It relayed the voices of such singers as Tetrazini, Melba, Patti and Caruso and the performances of well-known orchestras. The auxetophone, also known as a stentaphone, had actually been invented eight years earlier, but was a novelty to the general public. The famous conductor Sir Henry Wood is said to have been interested in this early amplifier, but his orchestra players complained that it would put musicians out of work since the amplifier increased sound so that one double bass would appear to produce the same volume as six. Relayed music proved very popular with Madame Tussaud's customers as they paraded through the halls.

A year later another novelty was presented, free of charge, in the form of 'a practically continuous, high-class cinematograph entertainment'. The north wing was converted into a theatre to hold 300 people where 'animated pictures of the highest order' were shown. Not since 1802 when Marie had shared the Lyceum Theatre with Philipstal's magic-lantern style Phantasmagoria had the wax exhibition shared a roof with another type of entertainment, curiously of a similar kind as if history were repeating itself. So the exhibition continued to develop, its fame and attraction undimmed by passing years. Here one could see reflected political and social changes, royalty, the arts, literature, and modern phenomena such as aviation. There were always new portrait figures of those in the public eye, and as far as visitors were concerned, the changing spectacle never palled.

By 1911 two of John Theodore's sons were working with their father. An era was about to come to an end in Europe but there were no signs of it here. In 1913 the Napoleon Rooms were redecorated in Empire style, green and gold, while two walls were panelled to frame pictures and screens erected to display smaller relics. In June 1914 the exhibition was re-arranged. The Hall of Kings was moved to a different area and was refurbished and improved, with new portrait figures of King George V and Queen Mary beneath an imposing canopy.

Just a matter of weeks later England was at war. John Theodore immediately started work on a huge war map modelled in high relief. It was installed in the entrance hall. This was always kept up to date and daily lectures given in front of it. In those days before radio or television many people came every day to listen to these war lectures.

On the outbreak of war attendance had declined for a while, but as the months passed the flow of visitors grew again. Khaki was now a dominant colour in the crowd as soldiers from overseas as well as British soldiers on leave wished to see the effigies of those they were fighting, as well as portraits of their own commanders. The Kaiser's effigy was attacked and mutilated many times! At one point it was removed, but soldiers in particular complained at not being able to gaze at the arch-enemy, so the Kaiser and several other enemy sovereigns were replaced in a special area and damage repaired as it occurred.

The doors of the exhibition were opened at eight o'clock in the morning, and there were always soldiers waiting for admission. Some were straight from the trenches with a few hours to kill before getting their leave-trains home. These often stumbled through the turnstiles and flung themselves on to an ottoman, or even on to the floor in some quiet area, and snatched a little sleep. They were never disturbed. In the cinema war films were shown and war relics were displayed to supplement the now thrice-daily lectures in front of the war-map. But the exhibition was not entirely given over to war. It was still a place for diversion and music. In 1917 a newspaper said that Madame Tussaud's exhibition was 'the most inexpensive and interesting entertainment in the Metropolis'. At Christmas there were special attractions and presents from Santa Claus for the children.

The Chamber of Horrors did not lack new inmates, one of the most notorious being George Joseph Smith, the murderer of 'Brides in the Bath' fame. He took his place accompanied by various 'relics' including one of the baths. Though John Theodore was sixty when the Armistice came in 1918, his energies had proved equal to sustaining the exhibition right through the war, while five of his sons served in the forces, one of them being taken prisoner after being shot down in an air battle.

In 1919 John Theodore began writing his reminiscences in a series of articles in the *Evening News*, and at the end of the year they were published in book form as *The Romance of Madame Tussaud's*. Queen Mary graciously accepted a copy. Her mother, the Duchess of Teck, had been a kind and interested patron of the exhibition and many Royal children and their parents had visited it.

The post-Great War years did not bring any spectacular changes. There were always new portraits, new groupings and new tableaux, as well as new candidates for the Chamber of Horrors. In 1923 John Theodore celebrated fifty years of modelling and *The Romance of Madame Tussaud's* went into a second edition. On 30 December Victor

Tussaud died aged eighty-two. A grandson of Marie, with vivid recollections of her, he had devoted his life to the exhibition, working till a late age on the publicity and arrangements for visitors. He had also been one of those responsible in 1884 for the Marylebone Road edifice. Victor was spared knowledge of the catastrophe that occurred fifteen months later. 1925 promised to be a normal enough year. The Royal Family group was re-clothed in new Court dress. Special features included a Parliamentary Group, a new 'Colonial Group', and one representing 'An Assembly of Notable Women', an attraction announced at the beginning of March. The blow fell soon after, on the night of 25 March. Fire broke out. It spread and the main exhibition was totally consumed in the flames. Only the Chamber of Horrors in the basement, though damaged by heat, smoke, and water, remained recognisable when the conflagration was finally quenched. Marie's lifetime dread had at last come to pass.

The cause of the disaster was never fully determined. It was thought the fire began through a fault in the wiring of the famous electric organ. Perhaps the firemen on night duty tried to quench the flames themselves, and did not call the fire brigade soon enough. Whatever caused it, the fire spread with terrifying rapidity. Madame Tussaud's went up in a holocaust that lit the London sky and was never forgotten by those who witnessed it. No lives were lost, but the damage was appalling. Bernard Tussaud, who was living in the country, wrote years later of what he saw when he arrived on the scene:

'As I joined my father, the late John Theodore Tussaud, white-faced and tense, who was directing operations, the position looked hopeless. All that remained of the work of my great-great-grandmother and her descendants was a pile of smoking rubble and twisted iron girders. It seemed as if Madame Tussaud's had vanished forever in a holocaust of flame.' The disaster seemed irretrievable. Yet something did remain of Marie's legacy. There was the inherited talent of her great-grandchildren and her great-great-grandchildren: there was the inherited tenacity that originally brought Marie to England and sustained her, alone as she was, through many years of hard work, travelling, shipwreck losses, reverses, and obstacles, until she had established herself and her sons in a unique position of international celebrity.

There was also the site, and the shell of the building. Most of the moulds from which the wax portrait heads could be re-made were stored in the basement and escaped serious damage. A nucleus of highly trained staff remained too. Two of these had worked in the exhibition for forty years, three for thirty years, two for twenty and one for fifteen years. Messages of sympathy, support and encouragement flowed in from all over the world. With talent, determination and know-how, as well as a still available location, Madame Tussaud's exhibition could, and would, emerge again on the London scene.

The remaining months of 1925 were consecrated to assessing, planning and taking decisions regarding reconstruction. In the summer of 1926 a new Company was formed and building work on a new exhibition started in November. The modern structure would include a cinema and a restaurant. Plans envisaged the making of no less than three hundred figures. Herbert Norris, well-known as an artist and art historian, was appointed to take charge of design, decoration, costumes, settings and arrangement.

While it was impossible in 1926 to reproduce the grandeurs of the 1884 building with 'Baron Grant's' marble staircase and Thornhill's painted ceiling panels, the new building would be worthy of its foundress, Marie Tussaud. There would be music and dancing in the restaurant and a Würlitzer organ in the cinema. John Theodore and his son Bernard were appointed chief modellers, and four of John Theodore's sisters continued to work in the wardrobe and studios. The tradition carried on. Marie's last surviving grandson, Francis Curtius, lived to see the new building nearing completion. Born in the year that the exhibition settled in Bazaar, Baker Street, he had worked in it, like his grandmother, almost from childhood, specialising in the colouring of the wax portrait heads. He had left when it ceased to be entirely a family business in 1889, devoting himself till his death at ninety-two to his interests of chemistry and electricity.

On Thursday 25 April 1928 the new Madame Tussaud's exhibition opened its doors. As many as possible of the living subjects of the portrait figures were invited, and many came including Sir Oliver Lodge, the physicist and psychologist, noted for his interest in spiritualism. Eight thousand visitors passed through the doors on the first day. The first film shown in the cinema was 'The Private Life of Helen of Troy'.

As on many occasions there was Royal approval. Queen Mary expressed gratification at the way her portrait figure was dressed. She had graciously given Herbert Norris permission to order a replica of one of her dresses from her own dressmaker. One of her ladies-in-waiting demonstrated to him on a lay figure exactly how the Queen wore her jewels. The Prince of Wales paid a visit incognito.

The exhibition continued its traditional course throughout the troubled thirties, reflecting the political and social climate, the arts and sport, adding new historical groups and tableaux. In 1933 the effigy of Hitler was smeared with red paint and a placard hung round its neck, 'Hitler the Murderer'. The figure was cleaned and put back in its place. Journalists were invited to celebrate the fifth anniversary of the re-opening with a supper in the Grand Hall and a tour of renovations. The Silver Jubilee of King George V and Queen Mary in 1935 was marked by special exterior lighting. When King Edward VIII abdicated his abdication speech was relayed throughout the exhibition and press pictures showed people crowded round the Royal Group as they listened to it.

A portrait of Mrs Wallis Simpson, the new King's friend and future wife, was added. The figure was placed on a dais near the Royal Group dressed in a red satin evening dress and 'ruby' jewellery specially made. She was not popular and an attendant was posted discreetly nearby in case anyone should attack the figure. The Coronation Group of King George VI and Queen Elizabeth was set up. In 1937 Bernard Tussaud appeared for the first time on television modelling and working on a new head of Neville Chamberlain.

John Theodore, Marie's great-grandson, celebrated his eightieth birthday. He bid fair to rival his ancestress, having made his first modelling essays at the age of five and devoting his life to the exhibition. The Munich crisis was looming and war threatening, but Madame Tussaud's did not stand still. In November up-to-date sound equipment was installed in the cinema. Famous personalities continued to be willing sitters, such as Anna Neagle, the actress, portrayed in her film role as Queen Victoria.

Time was running out and in 1939 preparations for war conditions began. It was decided no figures should be moved, but Bernard sorted out a number of moulds which were taken to the country for safe storage. When war was finally declared in September the portrait figure of Hitler was placed with a group of 1914/1918 enemy war leaders that was still on show. Bernard began to model Hermann Goering, and, as far as possible, the exhibition carried on normally. But for a time it seemed this war would do what even the disastrous fire had failed to do: close down Madame Tussaud's. The blackout, the evacuation of many Londoners and other war conditions caused attendance to fall drastically. However, the decision not to move out any figures, to keep the restaurant open and the band playing from 7 p.m. proved justified. As had happened in 1914 very soon the flow of visitors began to rise again. People adjusted themselves to war conditions and wanted entertainment, while soldiers on leave and from overseas made a visit to Madame Tussaud's exhibition a priority.

The early stages of the war were quiet and brought only minor difficulties. Bernard and his staff were working hard on portraits of war leaders and Ministers. Now sittings could hardly ever be granted. To supplement information gleaned from photographs Bernard and members of the studio staff became quite familiar figures, and accepted by the police, placing themselves at vantage points in Downing Street and Whitehall for the purpose of observation and note-taking. Medals and medal ribbons were a particular problem. One French general proved to have forty-three decorations and the help of the jeweller Cartier's house in Paris had to be enlisted. In the end all the war leaders managed to take their place correctly medalled.

In July 1940 John Theodore celebrated his eighty-second birthday by modelling a bust of Queen Mary in his own patented self-hardening clay. Still a dominant personality and full of energy like his great-grandmother Marie, he was destined to see another disaster befall the exhibition.

The Zeppelin raids of the Great War had left Madame Tussaud's unscathed, but Hitler's blitz was another matter. On the night of 9/10 September 1940 a direct hit completely destroyed the cinema, and badly damaged the restaurant. The wall of a mould store, whose contents had not been evacuated, collapsed and the moulds crashed into the crater, irretrievably smashed. Two hundred and ninety-five male head moulds and fifty-seven female were destroyed, many of them of historic interest.

Still Marie's luck, which had seen her and her exhibition through so many hazardous occasions, held. No lives were lost, no-one was even hurt. Though the effects of blast, dirt, rubble and broken glass closed the exhibition for some time, it was not seriously damaged. The news of the direct hit on Madame Tussaud's exhibition spread rapidly, and messages of encouragement came from all sides; King George VI and Queen Elizabeth honoured the exhibition by coming to Marylebone Road and inspecting the crater where once the cinema had stood. An incendiary bomb on 23 September did further damage but this was not severe. In December the exhibition re-opened, except the Hall of Tableaux which had suffered the worst effects of the blast. Once again troops on leave came in a steady flow.

As war continued restrictions became more stringent, difficulties multiplied. Clothes rationing brought acute problems. Madame Tussaud's exhibition was issued with a supply of clothing coupons, but this was totally inadequate as the modelling of new figures never halted. There were large stocks of clothes in the wardrobe but all too often these were unsuitable for dressing war-time personalities. Some 'subjects' helped out by giving some of their own clothing or parting with coupons. Soap rationing made cleaning the figures and washing the hair difficult. Fine curd soap had always been used, but now wardrobe and studio had to make do with an allocation of liquid soap.

On 13 October 1943 John Theodore Tussaud, Marie's great-grandson, died unexpectedly in his sleep at his home in Croxley Green. He had no illness and was active until the last. Perhaps of all her numerous descendants John Theodore came nearest to Marie in his splendid constitution, his vision, and his driving energy and determination. Almost his entire life, like hers, had been spent in the exhibition.

During the clearing out of the cellars of John Theodore's home after his death, a black box was found. It had apparently not been opened since Marie's sons, Francis and Joseph, brought it back from Paris after their father's death in 1848. It contained a number of legal documents relating to François's property dealings, some letters written by Curtius, the inventory of his country house at Ivry-sur-Seine, and a small bundle of letters written by Marie to her husband, from London, Scotland, and Ireland in 1803 and 1804 before she set out on her gruelling years of touring. John Theodore did not die a rich man, leaving only a few thousand pounds. Like his great-grandmother he had worked for the sake of the exhibition, not to amass wealth and property.

His son Bernard carried on, with a sister, Joan, looking after the wardrobe. Shortages grew more acute, one of them being a lack of natural hair which before the war had mainly come from Balkan countries. But ways were found and nothing was allowed to stand still. For Christmas 1943 there were new, more grown-up, portraits of Princess Elizabeth (now Queen Elizabeth II) and Princess Margaret. They wore blue gowns with a silver trim, which had been graciously chosen by the Queen, and made by Norman Hartnell, the Royal dressmaker.

When peace finally came to Europe in 1945 the exhibition geared itself, as it had always done, to meet the requirements of a changed world. The immediate post-war years brought no easing of immediate practical problems. In fact the modelling of an increased number of figures – a new Cabinet, a tableau group of VCs, additional sports and other personalities – made matters worse. Pre-war stocks of modelling necessities were practically exhausted. So depleted were stocks of glass eyes, especially blues and grays, which had originally been imported from Germany and Czechoslovakia, that at times it seemed choice of 'subject' for portraiture would have to be dictated by eye colour! It was a great relief when a manufacturer specialising in this product left the Continent to settle in London and set up business.

Even the establishment of the National Health Service brought about a near crisis. All available supplies of fine plaster, essential for making the moulds, were allocated to medical services. It was only when urgent representations were made, pointing out that Madame Tussaud's exhibition was of value to the nation as a tourist attraction and dollar earner, that sufficient of this material was released to the studio. Gradually things became easier. In 1949 the first Catalogue since 1942 was printed, paper supplies having been severely rationed. It was twice the size of pre-war Catalogues.

The centenary of Marie Tussaud's death in 1850 brought world-wide press coverage, and radio programmes. Her exhibition had survived Revolution, two global wars, fire, and bombing. Soon, with the death of King George VI, the ninth English monarch to be modelled, Queen Elizabeth II would take her place in the Royal Group. For the occasion the original manufacturers of the Throne Room carpet in Buckingham Palace were traced. The loom cards had survived and permission was given for a length of the Tudor rose pattern carpet to be woven to cover the dais. Two crystal chandeliers, copies of those in the Throne Room, were made. If not so lavish as Marie's King George IV tableau, the group was still impressive.

Plans were also under way for re-building on the bombed cinema site. This would not be replaced, but an entirely different project, the London Planetarium, the first of its kind in Britain, with equipment imported from Germany, was set up. The building was completed in 1958 and opened by the Duke of Edinburgh.

Marie's great-great-granddaughter Joan retired from the Wardrobe in 1962 and for some time Bernard was the only one of her descendants to work in the exhibition. He, with his late father John Theodore, had been modeller-in-chief since the new building rose from the ashes of the terrible fire in 1928. Drastic social changes had taken place since the War, and now Madame Tussaud's reflected the 'Swinging Sixties'. The Beatles group, modelled from life, caused great excitement. The Beatles attended the unveiling in person and attendances rose to record levels.

September 1966 saw the presentation of a new and impressive spectacular, the most ambitious in the exhibition's long history. Admiral of the Fleet Sir Philip Vian opened 'The Battle of Trafalgar'. This gave an accurate and full-scale representation of the port side of the Victory, with figures of some forty seamen manning four guns.

There was one great change from the past. Most of the figures were modelled in other media and only the portait of Nelson was in wax. He lay dying below on the orlop deck. Also the spectacle appealed to all the senses, with shafts of sunlight, the noise of collision, the flash and sound of gunfire, the smell on the air of smoke, gunpowder, tar and sea and the creaking sounds of a wooden ship afloat.

For a few years one of Bernard Tussaud's brothers had a seat on the Board, but early in 1967 he retired and Bernard was again the only one of Marie's descendants working in the exhibition. But not for long. In September Bernard died after a short illness at the comparatively early age of seventy-one. With his death the modelling talent inherited from Marie came at last to an end. There were no more of her many descendants trained and waiting to take over. Francis and Joseph, Joseph Randall, John Theodore and Bernard, all were gone.

But Marie's inspiration and the principles on which she had built, single-handedly, her great achievement, still remained. If she returned to the exhibition today, she would feel at home on familiar ground.

APPENDIX I

Madame Tussaud's Touring Years (1802–35)

Surviving press reports, posters, handbills, and catalogues give a remarkably comprehensive picture of Madame Tussaud's Exhibition during her long years of touring. Listed below are visits on which there is documentary information. Madame Tussaud seems to have taken few holidays, and from 1802 until she finally settled in London, touring was her life.

Alnwick: 1827
Bath: 1814; 1815; 1824; 1831
Belfast: 1808
Birmingham: 1813; 1822; 1823; 1831
Blackburn: 1822
Bolton: 1821
Boston: 1819; 1825; 1826
Brighton: 1822
Bristol: 1814; 1823; 1831
Burton-on-Trent: 1830
Bury St Edmunds: 1825
Cambridge: 1818; 1824
Canterbury: 1818; 1833
Carlisle: 1828
Chelmsford: 1825
Cheltenham: 1823
Chester: 1822
Cirencester: 1824; 1832
Colchester: 1824; 1825
Coventry: 1823; 1831
Cork: 1805
Deal: 1818
Derby: 1819; 1830

Doncaster: 1826
Dover: 1833
Dublin: 1804
Duffield: 1830
Dumfries: 1828
Durham: 1827
Edinburgh: 1803; 1810; 1811; 1828
Gainsborough: 1826
Glasgow: 1803; 1804
Gloucester: 1823; 1832
Grantham: 1830
Greenock: 1804; 1808
Hull: 1812; 1826
Ipswich: 1818; 1825
Kidderminster: 1822
King's Lynn: 1819; 1825
Kilkenny: 1805
Leamington: 1831
Leeds: 1812; 1820; 1827
Leicester: 1830
Lincoln: 1819; 1826
Liverpool: 1813; 1821; 1829
London: 1802; 1803; 1809; 1816; 1833; 1834; 1835

Louth: 1826
Maidstone: 1816; 1833
Manchester: 1812; 1813; 1820;
  1821; 1822; 1829
Newark: 1819; 1829
Newbury: 1816
Newcastle: 1811; 1827
Northampton: 1824
North Shields: 1811; 1812; 1827
Norwich: 1819; 1825
Nottingham: 1819; 1829
Oxford: 1824; 1832
Penrith: 1828
Peterborough: 1824
Plymouth: 1815
Portsmouth: 1815; 1830
Preston: 1822; 1828

Reading: 1816; 1832
Rochester: 1818
Salisbury: 1816
Sheffield: 1819; 1820; 1829
Shrewsbury: 1822; 1830
Stamford: 1824
Southampton: 1816
Stockton: 1827
Sunderland: 1827
Taunton: 1815
Wakefield: 1820
Warrington: 1822
Waterford: 1804
Worcester: 1814
Wigan: 1821
Yarmouth: 1825
York: 1812; 1826

APPENDIX II

The 1803 Biographical Catalogue

Seventy pages of the 1803 catalogue are devoted to the lives of Bonaparte, Carrier, Hébert, Marat, Mirabeau, Charlotte Corday, Robespierre, Frederick the Great, Benjamin Franklin, General Kléber, the Princesse de Lamballe and numerous others whose names are now forgotten. These sketches must have been dictated, or at least scrutinized, by Madame Tussaud, and they provide a guide to the opinions she voiced openly in this year when Napoleon was only beginning his conquests. He gets a good wigging for 'ambitiously planning' the invasion of England, and the 'overthrow of her people, their laws and their liberties'; Josephine has only one paragraph which calls her a 'woman possessed of great abilities of mind and body', but hints that her connection with Barras may not have been 'of the most honourable nature'. Carrier has the longest biography of all, and it presents his own defence for drowning and shooting, which is not uninteresting. Civil wars have always been noted 'for the reprisals made by one party upon another'. Charlotte Corday gets a eulogy. Marat is 'the enemy of the whole human race', and Robespierre 'affords a memorable instance of the effects of sudden elevation in debasing the human mind by making it ferocious. . . . He affected to be called a *Sans-Culotte*, but his clothes were always chosen with taste and his hair was constantly dressed and powdered with a precision that bordered on foppery'.

There is a short note on Madame de St Amaranthe, widow of a colonel of the Life Guards killed in the Tuileries confrontation. 'Robespierre in the height of his glory became enamoured of the lady's beauty, and importuned her to become his mistress, but, on meeting with a refusal, he ordered her head to be struck off by the guillotine.' Madame du Barry, 'elevated by accident from a brothel to a partnership in the throne', is suitably castigated, and the details of the end of the Princesse de Lamballe were certainly known to Madame Tussaud, for she mentions the perpetration of 'a thousand

107

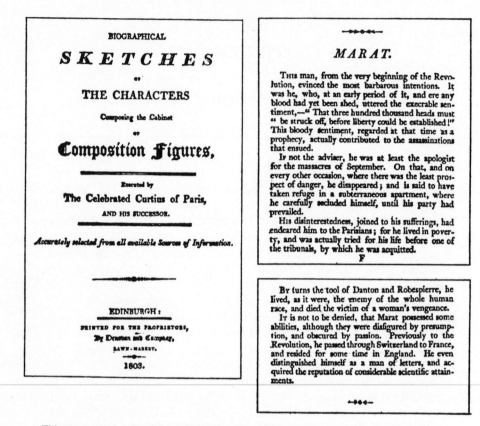

BIOGRAPHICAL

S K E T C H E S

ᴏꜰ

THE CHARACTERS

Composing the Cabinet

ᴏꜰ

Composition Figures,

Executed by

The Celebrated Curtius of Paris,

AND HIS SUCCESSOR.

Accurately selected from all available Sources of Information.

EDINBURGH:

PRINTED FOR THE PROPRIETORS,

By Denovan and Company,

LAWN-MARKET.

1803.

MARAT.

THIS man, from the very beginning of the Revolution, evinced the most barbarous intentions. It was he, who, at an early period of it, and ere any blood had yet been shed, uttered the execrable sentiment,—" That three hundred thousand heads must " be struck off, before liberty could be established !" This bloody sentiment, regarded at that time as a prophecy, actually contributed to the assassinations that ensued.

IF not the adviser, he was at least the apologist for the massacres of September. On that, and on every other occasion, where there was the least prospect of danger, he disappeared; and is said to have taken refuge in a subterraneous apartment, where he carefully secluded himself, until his party had prevailed.

His disinterestedness, joined to his sufferings, had endeared him to the Parisians; for he lived in poverty, and was actually tried for his life before one of the tribunals, by which he was acquitted.

F

BY turns the tool of Danton and Robespierre, he lived, as it were, the enemy of the whole human race, and died the victim of a woman's vengeance.

IT is not to be denied, that Marat possessed some abilities, although they were disfigured by presumption, and obscured by passion. Previously to the Revolution, he passed through Switzerland to France, and resided for some time in England. He even distinguished himself as a man of letters, and acquired the reputation of considerable scientific attainments.

Title page and extract from Madame Tussaud's Catalogue for her Exhibition in Edinburgh, May 1803. The educational aspect of the Exhibition is already emphasised. *Victoria and Albert Museum, London.*

barbarous and indelicate acts'.

The paragraphs entitled 'The Late Royal Family of France' explain how Curtius managed to keep this group until it was shown in the Trianon after the outbreak of the Revolution, and subsequently how Marie was able to bring it to England:

> The history of this unfortunate family is so well-known as to require no comment. The full length Portraits of the King, Queen, Princess Royal and Dauphin were taken by royal authority, to be sent as a present to the late Tippo Sultan a short time before the breaking out of the Revolution; the likenesses are equal to nature, and do much honour to Curtius. The commotion which took place in Paris prevented the King from putting his intention into effect – and the

Portraits remained concealed in the possession of Curtius and his successor until they were privately conveyed to this country.

The catalogue ends with three items: the shirt which Henry IV of France had been wearing when he was assassinated; 'the best conserved Egyptian Mummy ever seen in Europe'; and 'A model of the Original Guillotine, upon a scale of three inches to a square foot, accurately measured from that by which many thousand celebrated characters suffered in the Place de Grève at Paris'.

APPENDIX III

Chronology

1761   Anne Marie Grosholtz is born in Strasbourg, the posthumous daughter of Joseph Grosholtz, a soldier from Frankfurt, and Anna Maria Walder of Strasbourg. She is taken to Berne, where her mother acts as housekeeper to a German-born doctor and wax modeller, Philippe Guillaume Mathé Curtius.

1767   Marie is taken to Paris by her mother to join Dr Curtius, now established there as a successful wax modeller under the patronage of the Prince de Conti. Marie is taught wax modelling from a very early age.

1770   Curtius opens his first public wax exhibition in Paris.

1780   Marie, now a talented modeller in wax and working in Curtius's exhibition, is appointed art tutor to Madame Elizabeth, sister of Louis XVI. She goes to live at Versailles.

1789   Curtius calls Marie home to his house in the Boulevard du Temple in view of the political situation. On 12 July the mob seizes wax busts of Necker and the Duc d'Orléans from the exhibition. They are paraded through the streets, royal troops fire, and the first blood of the Revolution is shed. Curtius participates in the storming of the Bastille on 14 July.

1793   Louis XVI and Marie Antoinette are guillotined. Marie models their decapitated heads by command of the National Convention.

1794   Curtius dies at his country house at Ivry-sur-Seine, leaving Marie as his sole heiress. She continues to model and to manage the Exhibition in the Boulevard du Temple.

1795 Marie marries François Tussaud, a civil engineer from Macon.

1796 Marie's daughter is born, but dies in infancy.

1798 Marie's son Joseph is born.

1800 Marie's son Francis is born.

1802 After the Peace of Amiens, Marie decides to take her Exhibition to England, accompanied by her eldest son. She exhibits at the Lyceum Theatre, London.

1803 Marie takes her Exhibition to Scotland.

1804 Marie takes her Exhibition to Ireland. She decides not to return to her husband in Paris.

1808 Marie leaves Ireland for Scotland and England and starts twenty-six years of touring in both countries.

1835 Marie decides to settle permanently in London, with the Exhibition at The Bazaar, Baker Street/Portman Square.

1848 François Tussaud, Marie's husband, dies in Paris. They had not seen each other since her departure in 1802.

1850 Marie dies in London in her ninetieth year, leaving her Exhibition to her two sons, who in due course are succeeded by their descendants.

1884 Marie's grandsons move the Exhibition to a new, purpose-built building on the present site in Marylebone Road.

1889 Madame Tussaud's becomes a joint stock company but the family retain artistic direction and management.

1925 Madame Tussaud's Exhibition is almost entirely destroyed by fire. Rebuilding followed in 1926.

1928 The Exhibition re-opens with the addition of a cinema.

1940   Enemy action destroys the cinema, and damages the rest of the Exhibition, but it reopens within a short time.

1953   With the accession of Queen Elizabeth II, Madame Tussaud's presents the seventh Coronation Group in its history.

1958   The London Planetarium, on the site of the war-destroyed cinema, is opened by the Duke of Edinburgh.

1966   The beginning of a major rebuilding and improvement plan to update the 1928 post-fire reconstruction.

1967   Bernard Tussaud dies. Sculptor and great-great-grandson of Madame Tussaud, he was the last of her descendants to be directly associated with the Exhibition.

APPENDIX IV

The Salon de Cire
No. 20 Boulevard du Temple, Paris

The abiding influence in Marie Tussaud's life was that of Dr Philippe Curtius, sculptor in wax, her teacher and mentor, and his celebrated exhibition, the *Salon de Cire* at No. 20 Boulevard du Temple, Paris.

The official inventory of the contents of this large house, made shortly after his death in September, 1794, shows Curtius to have been not only a prolific artist in his medium, but also an avid collector of paintings, mirrors, furniture, 'relics', chandeliers and lamps, and bric-à-brac. He used these to make a grand and impressive setting in the rooms where his wax portrait figures and busts were displayed.

The inventory consists of eight closely written pages. The following extract from the listing of the contents of the Main Gallery gives an idea of the *Salon de Cire* as Madame Tussaud must have recollected it while she built up her own exhibition in England.

To give an idea of the enormous number of pictures, mirrors, chandeliers, and pieces of furniture collected by Curtius in his two houses and left to Marie on his death, the following is an extract from the eight-page inventory of No. 20 Boulevard du Temple. It is surprising to note in the inventory that no rooms in this Paris house seem to have been set aside as studios. Almost every room contained *some* wax figures and modelling material, and one has to presume that work was carried out in many corners. The fourteen-page inventory of the house at Ivry-sur-Seine gives the impression that not only had Curtius an eye for paintings, but he found the collection of furniture and *bric-à-brac* irresistible. Every room of this private country residence, as well as those of his large Paris house-cum-Exhibition, must have been overflowing. Had Marie managed to transport the contents of the houses she inherited to England, doubtless many treasures, as well as her own chairs from Versailles, would have reached her London Exhibition. This translation of one of the closely written pages of the inventory of No. 20 Boulevard du Temple in the autumn of 1794 gives an idea of the Main Gallery:

113

In a room on the ground floor giving on to the Boulevard, known under the designation of the Cabinet of Figures, the evidence is as follows: a large looking-glass in its frame adorned and decorated with crystal; another glass in two panels, in its frame of carved and gilded wood; another glass set in its panel of wood, another little glass in its frame of gilded beading; a glazed pottery stove with its copper flues; two little writing tables; two bench-seats stuffed with straw; another bench in Utrecht velvet; a velvet-covered dog-kennel; a square cashier's table covered in waxed cloth; three chairs with straw seats, a stool in Utrecht velvet; two branched wall-chandeliers and three copper candle-holders with crystal pendants; three lamps, each with three lights; three console tables in carved and gilded wood with marble tops; a clock in its case decorated with gilded copper; a barometer in its dial-case; two pairs of curtains in cotton material; two curtains in red serge; two pairs of large curtains in green taffeta; eight small muslin curtains; thirty-six pictures representing various subjects, painted in oils in their gold frames; 114 others, glazed in their gold frames; two more looking-glasses set in their panels decorated with gold mouldings; sixteen busts in their cases, each with three glass sides; nineteen other cases with glass panels, containing animals; twenty-nine other similar ones containing various objects; four more small tables; four side-tables three with copper gallery; another little table and two chairs stuffed with straw; a large mirror in the antique style, with its borders and capitals in glass with ornament of gilded wood; three large copper candlesticks; two tin candlesticks; one guitar; an Egyptian mummy in its case of painted wood; two cane chairs; four Argand lamps,* each with a single light; a small dressing-table; two pieces of glass not set in panels or frames; twenty-eight figures of large size, each clothed in its costume; ten other figures to the waist, also clothed; three other figures recumbent on beds; sixteen heads; an infant in its little chair with seat stuffed with straw, clothed; another little child, naked; two lanterns and two lamps; two flower-vases in blue glass; two large pictures painted on canvas; two more figures, one large-size, the other a bust, in their case with a glazed frame; and various other occasional objects.

---

* The name 'Argand lamp' was applied to a lamp and gas-burner invented by Aimé Argand (1755–1803). In France it was known as a *quinquet.*

Index